Lessons from the Zapatistas

ALSO IN THE CRITICAL DEVELOPMENT STUDIES SERIES

Lessons from the Zapatistas

From Armed Insurgency to Peoples' Autonomy

Expanded and updated English edition

**LIA PINHEIRO BARBOSA
& PETER M. ROSSET**

Translated from Spanish by Peter M. Rosset and Henry Veltmeyer

Foreword by James Schneider

critical development studies

FERNWOOD
PUBLISHING

Practical
ACTION
PUBLISHING

Copyediting: Erin Seatter
Cover Photo: Francisco de Parres Gómez
Cover Design: John van der Woude
Text Design: Lauren Jeanneau
Printed and bound in Canada

Originally published in Spanish as *Aprendizajes del Movimiento Zapatista: De la insurgencia armada a la autonomía popular* (2023), by Consejo Latinoamericano en Ciencias Sociales (CLACSO). Av. Callao 1020, 6to Piso, C1023 Buenos Aires, Argentina.
ISBN 978-607-876-7793.

Published in North America by Fernwood Publishing
2970 Oxford Street, Halifax, Nova Scotia, B3L 2W4
Halifax and Winnipeg
www.fernwoodpublishing.ca

Published in the rest of the world by Practical Action Publishing
27a Albert Street, Rugby, Warwickshire CV21 2SG, UK

Fernwood Publishing Company Limited gratefully acknowledges the financial support of the Government of Canada through the Canada Book Fund and the Canada Council for the Arts. We acknowledge the Province of Manitoba for support through the Manitoba Publishers Marketing Assistance Program and the Book Publishing Tax Credit. We acknowledge the Nova Scotia Department of Communities, Culture and Heritage for support through the Publishers Assistance Fund.

Canadä   Canada Council   Conseil des arts   NOVA SCOTIA   Manitoba
           for the Arts   du Canada

Library and Archives Canada Cataloguing in Publication
Title: Lessons from the Zapatistas : from armed insurgency to peoples' autonomy /
Lia Pinheiro Barbosa & Peter M. Rosset ;
translated from Mesonza by Henry Veltmeyer & Peter M. Rosset ;
foreword by James Schneider.
Other titles: Aprendizajes del movimiento Zapatista. English
Names: Barbosa, Lia Pinheiro, author. | Rosset, Peter, author, translator |
Veltmeyer, Henry, translator
Series: Critical development studies
Description: Expanded and updated English edition. |
Series statement: Critical development studies |
Includes bibliographical references and index. |
In English, translated from the Mesonza.
Identifiers: Canadiana 20250193000 | ISBN 9781773637532 (softcover)
Subjects: LCSH: Ejército Zapatista de Liberación Nacional (Mexico)—History. |
LCSH: Chiapas (Mexico)—History—Peasant Uprising, 1994- | LCSH: Social
movements—Mexico—History—20th century. | LCSH: Mexico—
Politics and government—1988-2000.
Classification: LCC F1256 .B3713 2025 | DDC 972/.75—dc23

Contents

We express our sincerest gratitude to the tireless struggle of the Zapatista peoples, who teach us every day about dignity as an ethical value and as a political principle in the struggle for autonomy, liberty and the unwavering defence of territories for life of people and our Mother Earth.

Critical Development Studies Series

Three decades of uneven capitalist development and neoliberal globalization have devastated the economies, societies, livelihoods and lives of people around the world, especially those in societies of the Global South. Now more than ever, there is a need for a more critical, proactive approach to the study of global and development studies. The challenge of advancing and disseminating such an approach — to provide global and development studies with a critical edge — is on the agenda of scholars and activists from across Canada and the world and those who share the concern and interest in effecting progressive change for a better world.

This series provides a forum for the publication of small books in the interdisciplinary field of critical development studies — to generate knowledge and ideas about transformative change and alternative development. The editors of the series welcome the submission of original manuscripts that focus on issues of concern to the growing worldwide community of activist scholars in this field. Critical development studies (CDS) encompasses a broad array of issues ranging from the sustainability of the environment and livelihoods, the political economy and sociology of social inequality, alternative models of local and community-based development, the land and resource-grabbing dynamics of extractive capital, the subnational and global dynamics of political and economic power, and the forces of social change and resistance, as well as the contours of contemporary struggles against the destructive operations and ravages of capitalism and imperialism in the twenty-first century.

The books in the series are designed to be accessible to an activist readership as well as the academic community. The intent is to publish a series of small books (54,000 words, including bibliography, endnotes, index and front matter) on some of the biggest issues in the interdisciplinary field of critical development studies. To this end, activist scholars from across the world in the field of development studies and related academic disciplines are invited to submit a proposal or the draft of a book that conforms to the stated aim of the series. The editors will consider the submission of complete manuscripts within the 54,000-word limit. Potential authors are encouraged to submit a proposal that includes a rationale and short synopsis of the book, an outline of proposed chapters, one or two sample chapters, and a brief biography of the author(s).

Acronyms

ACGAZs	Assemblies of Collectives of Zapatista Autonomous Governments
CAM	Coordinadora Arauco-Malleco
CCRI	Clandestine Revolutionary Indigenous Committee
CCRI-CG	Clandestine Revolutionary Indigenous Committee — General Command
CG-EZLN	General Command of the Zapatista Army of National Liberation
CGAZs	Collectives of Autonomous Zapatista Governments
CLACSO	Consejo Latinoamericano de Ciencias Sociales (Latin American Council of Social Sciences)
CND	National Democratic Convention
CNI	National Indigenous Congress
COCOPA	Commission for Concord and Pacification
CONAIE	Confederation of Indigenous Nationalities of Ecuador
EAZ	Zapatista autonomous education
ECOSUR	El Colegio de la Frontera Sur (The College of the Southern Border)
ESAZ	Zapatista Autonomous Secondary School
EZLN	Zapatista Army of National Liberation
FENOCIN	National Confederation of Peasant, Indigenous and Black Organizations
FLN	National Liberation Forces
FZLN	Zapatista National Liberation Front
GALs	Local Autonomous Governments
JBGs	Good Government Councils
MAREZ	Zapatista Rebel Autonomous Municipalities
NAFTA	North American Free Trade Agreement
PRI	Institutional Revolutionary Party
SERAZ	Zapatista Autonomous Rebel Education System

Introduction to the English Edition

The original version of this book was written in Spanish and published in Argentina and Mexico by the Latin American Council of Social Sciences (CLACSO) and the College of the Southern Border (ECOSUR), where it was somewhat of a bestseller. This edition has been translated into English, and we have updated it and expanded it with new material.

Why write a book about the Zapatistas in the Mexican state of Chiapas, near the border with Guatemala? Some people may remember the January 1, 1994, Zapatista uprising as a quintessential twentieth-century phenomenon, with little relevance to the different world we face in the third decade of the twenty-first century. Why would masked Mayan indigenous rebels' and their mestizo "rock star" *subcomandante*, "Marcos," who were splashed all over news networks in the mid 1990s, be relevant in a contemporary world facing multiple crises, with economic, social, environmental, climatic, health and spiritual-philosophical dimensions, not to mention the ever present spectre of a global fascist or neofascist far right?

Thirty years later, the Zapatistas are still very much with us, even if a two-decade media blackout imposed by the government of Mexico as part of a counterinsurgency strategy has made many forget them or think they have ceased to exist. Importantly, the inability or unwillingness of governments around the world to effectively address our civilizational and planetary crises has led many to lose faith in the very notion of *government* or the *state* — yet that is precisely how indigenous peoples across Latin American have felt since the European invasion more than five centuries ago. The Zapatistas have channelled our widespread loss of faith, not only with their proposal, but with their actual, real-world building of *autonomy* — autonomy from the state, or self-government.

Indigenous peoples tell us that during the 500-plus years since the Spanish, Portuguese, French and British imposition in the Americas of the Western concept and reality of the state, they have been decimated by physical and cultural genocide, had their land, territories and resources stolen and only become ever poorer and more excluded from mainstream society and economies. The Zapatistas point out that this exclusion and declining standard of living has now been extended beyond indigenous peoples to all of us, to all but the 1%, from Alaska and Canada to Tierra del Fuego, at the southern tip of South America, and in Asia, Africa, Europe and the Middle East. Between climate change, pandemics, migration, crime, poverty and a collapsing environment, the state is not only failing to save humanity and Planet Earth but is actively colluding with the capitalist corporate pillage and devastation of people and the planet. The state is *not* going to solve the problems of everyday people and the environment, not soon, and in fact, not ever, as it is part of the problem and not part of the solution.

But far from being anarchists in the tradition of European culture and politics, the Zapatistas have created their own hybrid ideology that draws on the millenary cosmovision of indigenous peoples, on the rich tradition of Latin American revolutionary thought, and yes, on Western currents of Marxism and even anarchism as well. The Zapatistas posit that if the state isn't going to solve our problems, then we must solve them ourselves. They have drawn on pre-colonial indigenous forms of collective, democratic self-government, in which everybody participates in "solving our problems ourselves."

Yet in a marked difference from other movements of indigenous peoples in the Americas and other continents, they are not calling for government by and for one ethnic group. Rather, they call for all peoples to come together to self-govern in what we have chosen to call *peoples', popular* or *radical* autonomy. We do that to distinguish Zapatista autonomy both from *ethnic* autonomy—which tends to privilege one ethnic group over others—and from *juridical* or *constitutional* autonomy, in which governments concede lukewarm, diluted, partial autonomy to regions or ethnic groups to pacify them and essentially bring them into the fold, into conformity with the larger capitalist model.

The idea of autonomy is of course controversial and polemical. We ourselves come from a background where we felt, from a leftist perspective, that the government or the state is where we should look to solve our problems and those of others, including those of the environment and the planet. Many still believe that. But it is not happening, and that is why we may simultaneously feel devoid of hope for the future yet constantly seeking new alternatives.

We believe that by studying and learning from the peoples' autonomy of the Zapatistas and from what we call Zapatista *critical theory*, or *critical thought*, we can gain new perspectives and ideas on how we can collectively address our civilizational crises. We are not suggesting that Zapatista autonomy is a formula or recipe that can be simply copied and replicated elsewhere or everywhere — of course that is impossible — but rather that their audacious example and ideas can challenge us to think outside the box, something that humanity urgently needs to do in this historical time. With that in mind, we humbly offer our interpretation of the lessons and inspiration we can all gain from the story of the Zapatistas.

After we finished updating this English language edition, the Zapatistas published important new communiques in which they announced philosophical changes accompanied by a material reorganization of their autonomy. To address this, we added a selection of these communiques as a "must read" postscript to this edition. With the postscript, this volume reviews how the Zapatistas began, what they have done, what they have learned, and where they are going. We hope that our readers enjoy the book and find it useful.

Lia Pinheiro Barbosa
Peter M. Rosset

Note

1   At first, as an armed clandestine movement, the participants wore masks to prevent the government from determining their true identities. They also used *noms de guerre*, or pseudonyms, to protect themselves from retaliation by the government. Over time, the masks became more of a symbol of struggle than a real need to assure security. They now function almost as the trademark of the Zapatistas.

En Movimiento [In Movement] Series of Small Books from CLACSO

The power of social movements stands out in recent history, particularly in the geography of Latin America. Different movements and, on occasion, real citizen rebellions have pushed for changes in the social and political times of this region. These struggles call into question, based on collective practice, the cleavages of persistent inequality and exclusionary, ecologically unsustainable models of development, as well as anemic democracy and strong authoritarianism. These struggles veto governments and policies, express demands that go beyond institutional channels, constitute collective identities, configure territories as resistances and existences, update experiences of transformation and take new steps forward, renew public debate and put society *in movement*. But mobilization is not the exclusive domain of popular sectors, nor of progressive forces and the left.

Collective actions of various kinds are also present in responses to the advances achieved by these struggles and in the experiences of progressive governments. The politics of the streets and the fields thus represents a significant element in the dispute for the future and demarcates the horizon of change. The Latin American Council of Social Sciences (CLACSO) makes available to readers this collection of small books on big topics that aims to give an account of the main social movements, revolts and conflicts in Latin America and the Caribbean in the twenty-first century. From different traditions of critical thinking and the social sciences, the En Movimiento library discusses the richness and prominence of these struggles and the paths of transformation they open.

Bernardo Mançano Fernandes
Julián Rebón
Series Editors, CLACSO
https://libreria.clacso.org/coleccion.php?c=48

Declaration of the Lacandon Jungle

The flower of the word will not die.
The hidden face of the
one who names it today
may die, but the word that came
from the depths of history and from the earth,
can no longer be uprooted
by the arrogance of power.

—First Declaration of the Lacandon Jungle

On the threshold of the twenty-first century, Latin America became the scene of a new cycle of popular, or peoples', struggles, many articulated by indigenous and peasant movements, in the face of the deepening of neoliberal policies in the region. In the crucible of this resistance, the armed uprising of the Zapatista Army of National Liberation (EZLN) erupted on January 1, 1994, under the slogan *Ya Basta!* (Enough Is Enough!), when thousands of indigenous peasants, with weapons in hand, occupied the municipal headquarters of six cities and towns in the state of Chiapas, in southeastern Mexico.

In San Cristóbal de las Casas, the EZLN offered its word to the world with the reading of the First Declaration of the Lacandon Jungle, a document that condenses the historical-political reasons for the armed uprising and that presents the eleven demands of the Zapatista Movement: work, land, shelter, food, health, education, independence, freedom, democracy, justice and peace. With the metaphor of the "long night of 500 years," the *faceless* announced their arrival and denounced the legacy of the conquest for indigenous peoples: the theft of their lands and territories, their cultural, political and economic subordination and their condemnation to historical oblivion in the framework of the modern, Western and capitalist nation-state.

By taking up arms, the Zapatistas took a stand against the North American Free Trade Agreement (NAFTA), denounced the extreme poverty in which indigenous peoples lived, demanded self-determination in their territories and recognition as holders of rights, and called Mexican civil society to a constituent assembly to draft a new constitution. The Zapatista political trajectory has been marked by different moments, from an initial attempt at dialogue with the state, with the San Andrés Accords, to a rupture and the announcement of radical autonomy in their territories with the creation of the *caracoles* (administrative centres of autonomous self-government) and the Good Government Councils (regional councils, known in Spanish as *Juntas de Buen Gobierno* [JBGs]). These would later bring international attention to autonomy as a strategy and a political project. And not just any autonomy — not ethnic autonomy, despite being an indigenous movement, nor constitutional or legal autonomy — but *radical, popular or peoples', class-based, self-declared* and *de facto autonomy* that neither asks for nor receives recognition from the state.

Three decades after the insurgency, Zapatismo offers the most complete, explicit and radical version of indigenous-peasant autonomy in the contemporary world. The central objective of this book is to analyze and summarize the conception and political praxis of Zapatista autonomy as a strategy and as the core of their defence of land and territory. We discuss the different facets or dimensions of autonomy in the construction of territorial self-determination and as a strategy of struggle at local, national and international levels.

Historical Background of Zapatismo

The armed insurgency of the EZLN was the result of a social amalgam typical of historical indigenous resistance in Mexico and in Chiapas in particular. It comes from a social fabric woven from the confluence of the following three historical, political and cultural forces in resistance: 1. indigenous political action based on collective identity and community-based social organization; 2. pastoral action based on liberation theology, with the potential for ideological articulation and political-cultural bonding; and 3. the emergence of an important political subject, exemplified by armed insurgents in resistance (Barbosa, 2015). At the end of the 1980s, these three forces constituted a historical bloc with a strong capacity for social pressure, in a period of political turmoil, culminating in the Zapatista uprising on January 1, 1994.

In this historical cartography of the Chiapas resistance, the 1974 Indigenous Congress of Chiapas, held in commemoration of the 400th anniversary of the birth of Fray Bartolomé de las Casas, stands out. The congress was a joint initiative of the government of the State of Chiapas and the Diocese of San Cristóbal de las Casas. However, a year before the event, an indigenous coordinating team took ownership of the organizing process and began to convene communities for participation in pre-congress regional meetings. Based on the Mayan tradition of dialogue and collective consensus, they held local plenary sessions to discuss and define the topics that would be addressed at the congress.

In this way, the Indigenous Congress of Chiapas assumed a multi-ethnic, multilingual character, becoming a propitious space for the formation of cultural and political forces, as well as a historical moment in which the political debate related to the problems that afflicted the indigenous communities was taken up and deepened. In the days of immersion in this debate, a political agenda was drawn up to articulate the main indigenous demands, to be presented in speeches in indigenous languages. According to Antonio García de León,

> It summed up the words of 250,000 Indians from 327 communities (out of a total of half a million who inhabited the state at that time), the words of a quarter of a million small streams that flowed

into rivers from the mouths of 1,230 delegates (587 Tzeltals, 330 Tzotzils, 152 Tojolabales, and 161 Choles) who, in an exercise of profound discussion, were able to produce unitary positions on four fundamental issues in the life of their communities, municipalities, villages and landscapes: land, commerce, education and health. The fifth theme, that of politics, had been censured by the Ladino organizers of the event, even though, without a doubt, it was the theme that all the colours were bathed in throughout the Congress. (1995, pp. 128–129)

Among the organizers of the 1974 congress, activists from diverse organizations from across Mexico participated, brought together by a political agenda of resistance and confrontation with historical political oblivion and disregard by the state. The presence of these organizations reinforced the character of rejection, public denunciation and repudiation of the so-called *indigenist* policy conducted by the Mexican state, particularly in Chiapas. This led the state government to withdraw its support for the congress, especially when it realized that it was becoming a space for the consolidation and strengthening of indigenous political forces. García de León (1995) states: "It was like the trunk of a tree with roots that were 500 years old and whose branches and leaves began to emerge right after, in a great variety of peasant organizations that were created with these same social bases in the main Indian and peasant regions of Chiapas" (p. 129).

The Indigenous Congress of Chiapas directly and indirectly influenced the armed uprising of the Zapatista insurgents. An element that stands out as one of the original strands of Zapatismo is liberation theology, especially the strand called *teología india* (Indian theology), led from below by the indigenous peoples of Chiapas and championed by the bishop of the Diocese of San Cristóbal de las Casas, Samuel Ruiz (Marcos, 2017). The much earlier First National Indigenous Congress, organized in the 1960s, and the Indigenous Congress of Chiapas in 1974, with the participation of Bishop Don Samuel, were spaces for gestation of the principles that would guide the Zapatista demands (Campa Mendonza, 1999).

The EZLN had already been formed and organized secretly since 1983, originally as the southern wing of a clandestine armed movement, the National Liberation Forces (FLN). However, it was not until the early 1990s that the debate began within the indigenous communities about whether the EZLN would declare war against the Mexican state, a decision that later led to its split from the FLN. During this period, indigenous peoples from all over the continent organized and promoted the 500 Years of Indigenous

Resistance campaign. Subcomandante Insurgente Marcos recounts how the process of defining the date for the armed uprising took place:

> In 1992 we perceived a very important issue for the indigenous communities, which was the character of the Conquest, what the *Discovery of America* meant, at that time when the 500th anniversary of the discovery was celebrated, with great festivities planned at the official level. Within the indigenous movement, I don't know if it was nationally, but at least locally, there began to be a kind of uneasiness about what that meant and the need to demonstrate, and finally they proposed that we should remember the 500 years as they really have been: as a continuous movement of resistance against domination. The process of radicalization had been precipitated, the peoples had reached a point of no return on the perspective of war that was expressed through the indigenous leaders, the heads of the communities and the regions that would later become *the Committee*. Then the indigenous leadership proposed that the war should begin in 1992. (Le Bot, 1997, p. 81)

With respect to the formation of the EZLN, the *subcomandante* points to three central aspects: "a political-military group, a group of politicized and highly experienced indigenous people, and the indigenous movement in the Jungle" (Le Bot, 1997, p. 52). In terms of the first aspect, Marcos was referring to the FLN, the Marxist-Leninist and Guevarist political-military group, composed of subjects from urban spaces, which believed that the political possibilities of peaceful struggle for change in Mexico were exhausted. For this reason, they were convinced that armed struggle was the only path, though they had no immediate plan to take up arms. Inspired by Ernesto Che Guevara's *foquista* legacy, they began the work of political-military organization, learning from Central American and South American guerrilla movements.

Marcos affirmed that the FLN believed it was necessary to form a political-military force that would be capable of

> confronting Power — by means of a people's war — defeat it, and establish a government towards socialism and the establishment of the dictatorship of the proletariat and communism. And in this sense, a guerrilla [little war] was proposed in terms very close to the *guerrilla foco*. (Le Bot, 1997, p. 52)

Lia Pinheiro Barbosa elaborates:

> In this political-military dimension, they characterized Mexico as a neocolonial country internationally dependent on the United States. They considered it necessary to form a national liberation movement to achieve a transition to democracy and socialism. This would be one of the reasons why, after this first moment of political-military organization, they named themselves the Zapatista Army of National Liberation — EZLN. (2015)

The other reason alludes to the tradition of Mexican resistance, related to the Mexican Revolution and the historical-political memory of peasant leader Emiliano Zapata, an icon of peasant struggle in the period of the Mexican Revolution of 1910. Zapata popularized the words "the land belongs to those who work it," and, under the slogan "Land and Freedom," he fought to win agrarian reform in Mexico, which ended up remaining a dead letter in the agrarian policy of the state of Chiapas, to which it arrived late and incomplete. The Plan of Ayala, written by Emiliano Zapata and Otilio Montaño in 1911, was a declaration of autonomy in the agrarian rebellion of the earlier Zapatista peasantry.

According to Marcos, "From the time of the War of Independence, we learned from the army of Morelos, and from the Revolution, especially from the Division of the North, from Villa, and from the Liberation Army of the South, from Zapata" (Le Bot, 1997, p. 59). In the symbolic plane, he explains, they took on symbologies of revolutionary movements, such as the colours red and black. In the case of the star, he said, it was the product of the encounter with the indigenous Mayan cosmovision, in which it represents human beings and their five parts: head, arms and legs.

The other two aspects of origin of the EZLN mentioned by the *subcomandante* — the group of politicized indigenous people and the indigenous movement of the jungle — result from the encounter between the first political-military expeditionary groups of the FLN and the local social fabric already generated during years of gestation of a peoples' movement in Chiapas, in which left-wing indigenous organizations participated, and the political-missionary action of liberation theology was carried out by the Diocese of San Cristóbal de las Casas in the region of Las Cañadas, Chiapas. In the process of organizing the 1974 Indigenous Congress, the diocese had invited Maoist groups, in particular the People's Union and later the Proletarian Line, to participate in the organizing work in indigenous communities. They stayed for a while in Chiapas, prior to the significant presence of the FLN, providing political training and forming organizations in the communities. Thus, Maoism is one of the precursors of Zapatismo. According to Adela Cedillo-Cedillo,

> What happened is that, as the positions of the liberation theologists and the political militants converged on the objective of emancipation of indigenous people, they found no contradiction between the word of God and armed struggle, which at some point [through the FLN] they came to consider as an effective mechanism of liberation. (2012)

The encounter with these cultural and historical-political forces converged in a second key moment: the split of the EZLN from the FLN, with a new EZLN structure, command and military hierarchy represented by the Clandestine Revolutionary Indigenous Committee (CCRI) and by the General Command of the Zapatista Army of National Liberation (CG-EZLN).

In a historical perspective, Pablo González Casanova (1995) points to a set of eight causes behind the rebellion in Chiapas: 1. the rebellious heritage of the indigenous Maya, including the Yucatecans and Guatemalans; 2. the production and profitability crisis of the traditional hacienda economy; 3. Catholic pastoral action; 4. the student movement of 1968; 5. the failure to implement land reform, which meant *less land for the poor*; 6. a process of politicization of indigenous peoples through multiple organizational experiences; 7. the historical institutional violence exercised by the state of Chiapas and the absence of the rule of law; and 8. "negotiated violence with losses and gains."

Marcos explains that the war announced by the EZLN and indigenous peoples went beyond a political revolution such as those carried out in the past and in the more recent history of Mexico:

> The idea of a more just world, everything that socialism was, in broad strokes, but transformed, enriched with humanitarian, ethical and moral elements, more indigenous. Suddenly, the revolution became essentially moral. Ethical. More than just the distribution of wealth or the expropriation of the means of production, revolution began to be the possibility for human beings to have dignity. Dignity is starting to be a very strong word. It is not a contribution of ours, it is not a contribution of the urban element, this was contributed by the communities. The revolution became the guarantor that dignity be fulfilled and respected. (Le Bot, 1997, pp. 60–61)

Nevertheless, analyzing the antecedents of Zapatismo, we observe that its complexity makes it difficult to define it solely as an indigenous social movement or a guerrilla movement. As a socio-political phenomenon, it encompasses cultural, social and political elements of the tradition of Mexican peasant-indigenous resistance, of Latin American revolutionary struggles, with a theoretical base strongly inspired by Marxist-Leninist-Guevarist-Maoist contributions and an interpretative-epistemic view of the Mexican and Chiapas socio-political reality informed by the Mayan indigenous worldview. For these reasons, Christopher Gunderson (2017) describes Zapatista political ideology as a "provocative cocktail."

From Negotiation with the State to Radical Autonomy

The national and international public repercussions of the political demands of the First Declaration of the Lacandon Jungle, read on the night of the armed uprising and the announcement of the war, led Mexican and international civil society to hold public events demanding a ceasefire by the Mexican army. Two weeks after the start of the armed conflict, the federal government announced a ceasefire, and a period of negotiation began between the two parties. Based on the set of rights endorsed by the International Labour Organization's Indigenous and Tribal Peoples Convention, 1989 (No. 169), the following five thematic sessions were originally planned to guide the process for the achievement of a peace agreement: 1. Indigenous Rights and Culture; 2. Democracy and Justice; 3. Well-being and Development; 4. Reconciliation in Chiapas; and 5. Women's Rights in Chiapas.

On March 1, 1995, in conjunction with the Legislative Commission for Dialogue and Conciliation, the Federal Executive announced the bill for Dialogue, Conciliation and Dignified Peace in Chiapas. This document was sent on March 6 to the Congress of the Union for discussion and was approved unanimously. The law entered into force on March 11, 1995, creating the Commission for Concord and Pacification (COCOPA), a bicameral legislative commission composed of members of the Senate and Chamber of Deputies of Mexico. COCOPA would facilitate the negotiation process between the government and the EZLN.

For the Zapatistas, the opening of the negotiations was an important process of political articulation with national and international civil society. It represented the materialization of a dialogue built on the communiqués, letters, stories and other publications of the movement, as well as a series of events convened by the EZLN to collectively analyze the Mexican political situation and, particularly, the political proposal of the Zapatista Movement.

Throughout 1994 and 1995, the EZLN summoned the Zapatista communities and representatives of civil society to participate in three important events (two of them organized as plebiscites). The first, born out of the

13

Second Declaration of the Lacandon Jungle, was the National Democratic Convention (CND). The CND was a call to Mexican civil society to participate in the process of building new political relations, based on the principles of democracy, freedom and justice. The first plenary meeting of the CND was held in August 1994, in the Zapatista territory of Guadalupe Tepeyac, with the participation of approximately 7,000 people. There, the EZLN announced the formation of a peaceful national movement, breaking with the traditional Mexican political structure, and calling on civil society — "in whom our sovereignty resides" — to organize and join the process of building a "free and democratic space for political struggle" (EZLN, 1994).

In a continuous dialogue with civil society, the first popular plebiscite (neither asked for by, nor received recognition from, the state) — the Consultation for Peace and Democracy — was convened by the National Coordinator of Civic Action-National Liberation to consult with the public on the eleven demands by the EZLN in its First Declaration of the Lacandon Jungle. The second popular plebiscite, the National and International Consultation for Peace and Democracy, also convened by the EZLN, articulated the themes that would be the focus of the working groups for dialogue with the government. In both consultations, the EZLN demonstrated its ability to convene Mexican and international society. The numbers are emblematic: 1,300,000 in the national segment of the consultation and approximately 60,000 in the international segment, including participation from twenty-eight countries (Barbosa, 2015).

With respect to the consultations carried out by the EZLN, the Zapatista communities stressed that three central aspects were missing in the proposals for the Accords: "(1) a solution to the serious national agrarian problem as a result of the reform of Article 27 of the Constitution; (2) legal recognition of local and regional self-government; 3) solution to the demands on the right to information, justice and political rights."[1] For the EZLN, the processes of popular consultation at the internal level — with the Zapatista communities — and at the external level — in the dialogue with other political actors of national and international civil society — constituted an important democratic exercise. A communiqué issued in February 1996 by the CCRI-CG stated:

> The consultation of the Zapatista support bases is not only a democratic exercise within the EZLN, it is the foundation of the legitimacy of our organization and the guarantee of following the interests of the people and not the interests of individuals or groups. (Palabra, 2011)[2]

To generate a space for reflection and debate about these elements, in 1996, the EZLN announced the creation of the Aguascalientes: Aguascalientes I (La Realidad), Aguascalientes II (Oventik), Aguascalientes III (La Garrucha), Aguascalientes IV (Morelia) and Aguascalientes V (Roberto Barrios). The name "Aguascalientes" refers to the revolutionary constitutional convention that met in the city of Aguascalientes on October 10, 1914. The Aguascalientes convened in 1996 served as centres of resistance and spaces for the political and cultural activities of the Zapatistas in their dialogue with Mexican and international civil society. For example, the dialogue in 1996 included the following events: National Indigenous Forum, II National Meeting of Civil Committees for National Dialogue, Special Forum for State Reform, and Intercontinental Meeting for Humanity and against Neoliberalism (Barbosa, 2015).

On February 16, 1996, the EZLN and the federal government signed the San Andrés Accords on Indigenous Rights and Culture, which included the first thematic session, Indigenous Rights and Culture. As a result of this agreement, the Mexican government promised to amend the Mexican Constitution to grant indigenous rights, including those referring to the elaboration of a constitutional framework for autonomy of the indigenous peoples of Mexico, expressed in the following articles:

> 157. The right to self-determination and autonomy of indigenous peoples is recognized, as communities with a different culture and with the capacity to decide their fundamental affairs within the framework of the national State.

> 158. Recognition of the autonomy of indigenous peoples will be promoted, in accordance with the additions and amendments to the General Constitution of the Republic.

> 159. The recognition of the multicultural composition of the State of Chiapas, which is originally based on the existence of its indigenous peoples, will be promoted, understanding by indigenous peoples those who, having a historical continuity with the societies prior to the European irruption, maintain their own identities and the will to preserve them, based on a territory and on their own and differentiated cultural, social, political and economic characteristics. (Aubry et al., 2003, pp. 81–82)

The EZLN managed to put the issue of autonomy on the negotiating table as a core project for the construction of a new Mexican state (Barbosa, 2015). In the context of the San Andrés Accords, the Zapatista demand for the right to autonomy implied the inclusion of indigenous peoples as citizens with equal constitutional rights while at the same time respecting the right to self-govern, self-manage their territory and natural resources, and preserve their culture, language, and customs. The slogan "Never again a Mexico without us" was an expression of this Zapatista demand.

According to Barbosa (2015), the attempt at dialogue between the EZLN and the Mexican government had two important dimensions. The first was the political essence of the San Andrés Accords, that is, the legitimacy of the political demand for the constitutional recognition of the collective rights of indigenous peoples. Second, the recognition of the San Andrés Accords was a symbol of the Zapatista political struggle for indigenous rights. In this sense, the thematic sessions proposed in the negotiations transcended the horizons of the set of demands presented in the First Declaration of the Lacandon Jungle, especially because they situated the debate on indigenous rights within the framework of the construction of an autonomous project for the original peoples of Mexico.

The Zapatistas demanded an end to the persecution, repression and violation of human rights in the Zapatista communities and support bases, in addition to the withdrawal of the military camps and bases from the indigenous territory of Chiapas and the release of political prisoners. As well, the EZLN announced that the continuation of the dialogues of San Andrés was conditional on the state's compliance with the first agreement, in the sense of assuming a commitment to respect the indigenous peoples and implementing the signed agreements.

However, the proposed law and constitutional reform finally presented by the government did not incorporate much of the essence of what was agreed upon in the Accords. The government's failure to institutionally validate what was agreed at the first discussion table was a clear demonstration of political disinterest on the part of the Mexican state. In Zapatista words, it was a *betrayal*. This led to the Zapatistas withdrawing from the negotiations, the suspension of the other thematic sessions, and the taking up of radical autonomy, *without the state*, as a political project.

The decision taken by the Zapatistas led to the process of implementing the principles of the San Andrés Accords via the voice and hands of the rebellious indigenous peoples, who began the long and arduous journey towards the construction of their own autonomous structures. In this process, democracy was strengthened *from below* within indigenous communities. Central to this process was the placement at the centre of public debate a historic national problem: the denial of the right to political participation and self-determination of the indigenous peoples of Mexico.

For this reason, it was essential to underline the right to autonomy in the following four dimensions: 1. legality: to clearly include in the law the recognition of the rights of indigenous peoples, above all, the right to self-determination; 2. politics: the construction and consolidation of truly democratic channels and processes with broad popular participation, including that articulated by the indigenous peoples; 3. gender: incorporating indigenous women as a constituent part of the construction of the autonomous project; and 4. decolonization: recovering and strengthening the underlying referents of the Mayan cosmovision or worldview, culture, and language in the internal sphere of the Zapatista communities (Barbosa, 2015).

To support the expression and materialization of a long historical process of resistance by indigenous peoples throughout Latin America, Zapatismo clearly highlighted the following in the Third Declaration of the Lacandon Jungle in 1995:

> The indigenous question will not be solved if there is no RADICAL transformation of the national pact. The only way to incorporate, with justice and dignity, indigenous people into the nation is to recognize their own characteristics in its social, cultural and political organization. Autonomies are not separation; they are integration of the most humiliated and forgotten minorities in contemporary Mexico. This is how the EZLN has understood it since its formation, and this is what the indigenous bases that make up the leadership of our organization have mandated. (EZLN, 1995a)

In 1998, autonomy more clearly came to underlie the Zapatista political project with the creation of the Zapatista rebel autonomous municipalities. A fundamental fact in the process of building the Zapatista autonomous project was the transition from the condition of "municipalities in rebellion" to the proclamation of "rebel autonomous municipalities," which came to be known as the MAREZ. Three moments heralded the creation of the MAREZ (Barbosa, 2015). The first was the Peace with Justice and Dignity Campaign for Indigenous Peoples, carried out in 1994, as a denunciation of the military presence in the areas with Zapatista bases of support. The purpose of the campaign was to peacefully break the government's military siege, and it culminated in the advance of Zapatismo into new indigenous territories.

At this time, thirty municipalities declared themselves "municipalties in rebellion," and these indigenous communities created "rebel municipal councils," initiating self-government based on the Zapatista principle of *mandar obedeciendo* (commanding by obeying), a process that began in 1996 with the breakdown of dialogue with the Mexican government. The following is one of the pronouncements issued by a municipality in rebellion:

> We want to tell everyone that we indigenous people are here. Despite the total militarization of our communities, we resist. Not even with their warplanes will they be able to destroy the hearts of our people, because we follow the advice of our grandparents, and we are like the wind, *Ik'Otik* …. The creation of our Tierra y Libertad municipality and the formation of our municipal council is by our decision and by our strength, and our decision is backed by the Constitution and by the San Andrés Accords signed by the federal government and the EZLN. Our peoples have made the decision …. We, as indigenous peoples, have decided to govern ourselves with freedom, democracy and justice, and we have formed our municipalities and democratically appointed our authorities. Our legality therefore comes from the Mexican Constitution and the San Andrés Accords signed by the Mexican government in February 1996. (EZLN, 1998a)

A 1995 communiqué issued by the CCRI-CG of the EZLN declared that the autonomous municipalities would be governed under the principle of commanding by obeying and in conformity with the following laws: "1. The Political Constitution of the United Mexican States of 1917; 2. The Zapatista Revolutionary Laws of 1993; 3. The local laws of the municipal committee that will be determined by the civil will" (EZLN, 1995b, p. 182).

The second moment in which autonomy was declared came in 1996, when the EZLN expressed its disagreement with the electoral processes carried out for mayors in the municipalities of Chiapas. This conjuncture of political discontent had begun a year earlier, when the EZLN called on the Zapatista support bases to not participate in the elections, which resulted in the majority presence of the Institutional Revolutionary Party (PRI) in the mayors' offices of the Chiapas municipalities.

The third moment occurred after 1997, on the occasion of the aforementioned non-compliance with the San Andrés Accords by the Mexican government. The EZLN announced its withdrawal from the discussion and dialogue sessions. It began the process of consolidating its autonomy project in a collective effort to consolidate an *other* democracy within the indigenous communities, the Zapatista support bases.

The concept of *free municipalities* is absolutely linked to the indigenous tradition of self-government of their territories. In this form of self-management, local self-governments are conceived as collegial structures for integration into municipal councils. These municipalities are structured around three axes: 1. the right of indigenous communities to elect their traditional and municipal authorities in accordance with their uses and customs, granting legal validity to their institutions and practices; 2. participatory democracy as the foundation of the political exercise; and 3. the capacity of association between municipalities for the development of regionalized actions, which allows them a greater and better use of the territory and resources, increasing the management and development capacity of the municipalities (Agosto, 2006).

Since its origins, Zapatismo has had two command structures: a civilian one, represented by the Clandestine Revolutionary Indigenous Committee–General Command (CCRI-CG) and a military one, the Zapatista Army of National Liberation (EZLN). All functions are assumed from the system of *cargos*,[3] which are attributed by the local assembly and carried out during a certain period. With the announcement of the new stage of consolidation of autonomy in 2003, a reconfiguration of the Zapatista territory took place, with the creation of the *caracoles* (literally translated as "snails,"), the good government councils (JBGs) and the structuring of autonomous government (Marcos, 2003). These are represented 1. at the local level by autonomous agents and commissioners, who are the authorities in each community; 2. at the municipal level by the authorities of the municipality responsible for orchestrating the dynamics of community life in the communities that make up the autonomous municipality; and 3. in the region by the JBG, with one located in each *caracol* (Barbosa, 2015; 2016).

In the political structure of the MAREZ, the highest authority is the autonomous council, made up of a municipal president (councillor), vice president (alternate councillor), treasurer, secretary, judge, syndic and agent of communal property, as well as committees on education, health, sanitation, water, electricity, and vigilance. Likewise, along with the civic authorities is a council of elders, made up of women and men who have fulfilled all the positions assigned to them by the communities (Martínez Cuero, 2013).

Since its public appearance, Zapatismo has developed its own way of expressing itself and communicating publicly in what might be called an "aesthetics of resistance" (Barbosa, 2015; 2019), marked by a symbolic territoriality of an ontological and epistemic nature, rooted in Mayan philosophical thought. The very word *caracol*, "snail" — *puy* or *tot* — refers to representations in the Mayan cosmovision (Aubry, 2003). *Caracol* is linked symbolically to the cyclical indigenous conception of time, as opposed to the linear Western view of history. We find the symbolism of the *caracol*, or snail, in Mayan codices, in sacrifices made to the gods in the rites of puberty, fertility, childbirth and birth, since it is the symbol of the lunar goddess Ixchel, deity of procreation, marriage, medicine, water and land (Barbosa, 2019). The *caracol* is also an instrument (conch) used to summon residents to community assemblies, that is, an invitation to collective dialogue and participation in community life. For the elderly, it represents leaving their interiority to enter the heart of the other, that is, the dialogic communication that is established on a spiral path, in a continuous movement that is both endogenous and exogenous. In the same way, it represents the slow pace of the snail, which symbolizes the unhurried process of building channels of communication, dialogue and debate among the Zapatista communities until a consensus is reached (Barbosa, 2019; 2015).

During the First International Colloquium *in Memoriam* Andrés Aubry, in 2007, Subcomandante Insurgente Marcos emphasized the meaning of the *caracol* in Zapatista territories: "The *caracol* in our villages is how the collective is summoned. When the men are in the cornfield and the women are at work, the caracol summons them to meet in an assembly and it is then that they become a collective. That is why we say that it is the "Caller of the We" (EZLN, 2007b, pp. 318–19).

In 2003 there were five *caracoles*, and these were expanded in 2019 with eleven more, now also called Centres of Autonomous Resistance and Zapatista Rebellion.[4] All levels and organs of self-government are collective and rotating (Starr et al., 2011). The JBGs are the administrative hearts of the *caracoles*. The JBGs are made up of one or two delegates from the autonomous councils of the MAREZ, who are elected by an assembly for a two-year term of unpaid community service. They are responsible for coordinating a certain number of MAREZs and carrying out the following functions (Burguete Cal y Mayor, 2005; Barbosa, 2015): coordinating, promoting and monitoring the social projects developed in the MAREZ; allocating the support funds that enter the MAREZ, on which a 10 percent tax is charged; administering justice and security; facilitating activities related to production, trade and local transport; working to reduce imbalances within the MAREZ; mediating conflicts between the MAREZ and non-Zapatista municipalities and communities; regulating membership, rights and obligations; regulating the entry of visitors, researchers and others into the MAREZ; monitoring compliance with agreements; dealing with complaints against the autonomous councils (investigating, problem solving and punishing if needed); dealing with complaints of human rights violations by the military or paramilitaries; and dialoguing with all those who come to the *caracoles* to learn about the Zapatista Movement, whether they are Mexicans (called "nationals" by the Zapatistas) or foreigners (internationals), whether linked or not to international solidarity networks.

Almost all the issues that go through the JBGs are channelled to the community assemblies. The JBGs can also request the creation of peace camps and human rights observatories in the MAREZ, among other activities that can be carried out in Zapatista territory. It is worth noting that most of the political work is carried out by those in charge of the movement at the communal and municipal levels, in the fields of jurisprudence, education, production, health, land, trade, culture and justice, among others (Barbosa, 2015).

The work of the JBGs is overseen by the CCRI-CG to avoid any act of corruption, arbitrariness, injustice, intolerance and deviation from the Zapatista principle of commanding by obeying. This principle is directly related to the Zapatistas' form of political participation, the construction of a grassroots democracy, in which the people give their voice to the representative bodies within the movement — JBGs, autonomous councils, CCRI-CG — so that they command but in obedience to the peoples' consensual decisions taken in assemblies (Baronnet, 2010; Baronnet et al., 2011; Brancaleone, 2015; EZLN, 2013a; Esteva, 2014; Marcos, 2003; Mora, 2017; Stahler-Scholk, 2007; Starr et al., 2011).

In the process of structuring the autonomous government, the Zapatistas have built a "rebellious ethic" that sustains horizontality in the construction of a grassroots democracy and that is based on the seven Zapatista principles:

1. *Obedecer y No Mandar* (To Obey, Not Command)
   This Zapatista principle emphasizes the importance of executing the will of the people, while holding a position of leadership. In Zapatista autonomous communities, leadership positions are short-lived. This reflects the need for leaders to obey the collective desires of the community rather than command them from a position of power.

2. *Proponer y No Imponer* (To Propose, Not Impose)
   Humility is a key part of life for the Zapatistas and aligns with their practice of debate and self-reflection. This principle is birthed from the Zapatista culture of proposing a path forward and not imposing one.

3. *Representar y No Suplantar* (To Represent, Not Supplant)
   Deriving from the Zapatista understanding that before the colonizer arrived, indigenous people governed themselves. This principle is guided by the importance of self-governance and is grounded in the collective trust of the community to represent what the community wants.

4. *Convencer y No Vencer* (To Convince, Not Conquer)
   The principle to convince not conquer is important to the practice of dialogue and assembly. For the Zapatistas, convincing requires logical argument, reflection, consideration of many viewpoints, and open discussion.

5. *Construir y No Destruir* (To Construct, Not Destroy)
   The fifth principle is rooted in an ethic of anti-destruction and an end to exploitation. This principle is a practice in creating the institutions and the world that we want. This includes the unique Zapatista view of both relationships to humans and the land.

6. *Servir y No Servirse* (To Serve Others, Not Serve Oneself)
   A traditional value for the indigenous people of Chiapas is humility. The Zapatista slogan, "Para todos todo, para nosotros nada" (Everything for Everyone, Nothing for Ourselves), is at the core of this principle. Every Zapatista must find a balance in serving others for the collective while taking care of their individual family work.

7. *Bajar y No Subir* (To Work From Below, Not Seek To Rise)
   In Zapatista communities collective work is a way of life. This principle aligns with the mentality of working at the grassroots level for the benefit of the community.

These seven principles articulate a historical legacy of Mayan cosmovision and are expressed from a double dimension: they are born from experience, and, at the same time, they are seeds for this same experience. They provide a philosophical-epistemic matrix, constituting a rationality that is transversal in the political praxis of construction and consolidation of the political project of autonomy.

   An extremely important aspect in the framework of the construction of Zapatista autonomy is that the *caracoles* do not receive (nor do they accept) any type of material or financial resources from state institutions and political parties. Budgets in the Zapatista zone come from national and international donations, from self-taxes and collective production, and/or from projects carried out in the communities and support bases. All the structures built in the *caracoles* and/or MAREZ are the result of the voluntary work of indigenous communities, along with national caravans of support and international solidarity.

In the consolidation of their political project, the Zapatistas specify seven axes of what they call "autonomous resistance" (EZLN, 2013d): economic resistance, ideological resistance, psychological resistance, cultural resistance, political resistance, social resistance and resistance to the military and paramilitary presence. Each of these axes, which we discuss throughout this book, sustains the exercise of autonomous government in the Zapatista territories.[5]

In three decades, several dimensions of Zapatista autonomy have become palpable: self-government, autonomous education, autonomous community health, autonomous agrarian reform, agroecology, autonomous justice and community self-defence, autonomous communications and culture, economic organization in the communities, in the autonomous regions and even inter-regionally, and collective work, as well as the significant participation of women and youth. In collective work, there are local collectives responsible for working in the cooperatives and shops, planting crops, caring for livestock and maintaining local security, information and culture, among other activities. It is striking that all the tasks assumed within the structure of the autonomous government, as well as in the other aspects of autonomy, are carried out without receipt of any salary, but instead by commitment to all the activities that are linked to the material and socio-cultural reproduction of life in their territories.

The Zapatista women constitute a collective historical-political subject that has been at the centre of the processes described above. They were the ones who demanded that the communities take up arms when the men doubted whether there was a favourable correlation of forces; the women were responsible for a revolutionary law before the uprising; and today they are at the heart of autonomy.

Notes

1   Results of the consultation with the Zapatista rank and file can be consulted in Table 1, on indigenous rights and culture, in Palabra (2011).

2   In the Zapatista lexicon, the phrase "bases of support," or "support bases," refers to the civilian population in the territory that recognizes the Zapatista structure as its legitimate form of government.

3   A "system of *cargos*" refers to the typical governance and spiritual structure of indigenous communities, which has no easy translation to English. It is a rotating system of political and spiritual communal obligations and responsibilities, which are assigned by the collective and taken on by individuals as unpaid service to the community. The word *cargos* refers to the different positions held by different people at different times within the community service structure.

4   Note that this structure underwent significant modifications after the Spanish edition of this book was written, as described in the Postscript to this English language edition.

5   It is important to note that Zapatista territories and territorialities in a large part of Chiapas overlap with those belonging to what they call the Mal Gobierno ("Bad Government"). Thus, the same village can easily have both Zapatista families, who answer to the MAREZ and their autonomous municipal government, and non-Zapatista families, who answer to the official municipalities. Such villages often have two schools, one autonomous and one official, two clinics, one autonomous and one official, one autonomous pharmacy, and both private pharmacies and public ones belonging to the Bad Government. And what happens, many times, is that the official clinic will have neither a doctor nor nurses, nor medicines in their pharmacy. Non-Zapatista families often go to the Zapatista clinic and pharmacy, where everything is free for Zapatista families, but where non-Zapatista families pay a small, symbolic cost to use the service. This possibility for non-Zapatistas is part of Zapatista pedagogy towards society, which tries to demonstrate the benefits of autonomy.

Without Women
There Is No Revolution!

As the women we are ...
We also have words, ideas
to analyze, to see problems.

—Comandanta Dalia. (EZLN 2015a)

The winds prior to the armed insurgency of the EZLN brought the early morning mist of the female presence of indigenous women who, in March 1993, led the "first insurgency," making public in an unexpectedly surprising way what would be the first revolutionary law of the Zapatista Autonomous Justice System: the Revolutionary Law of Women. Throughout this political trajectory, Zapatista women have shared the historical background of the indigenous situation in Chiapas before 1994 and, in particular, the oppressive conditions faced by indigenous women. At the 2007 Zapatista Women's Meeting with the Women of the World in Caracol III — La Garrucha, a Zapatista woman recounted:

> He had us like animals. There came a day when the landowner ordered his men to go and grab the girls, so that they could rape them. That's what the landowners did. He saw to it that all the girls were raped. All the girls, not just one or two. I don't know how many girls passed through their hands. (zz colectivo, 2012)

In the context of colonization marked by profound racism, sexual violence represents a recolonization of indigenous women's bodies. It attributes to them the character of a territorial extension circumscribed by the colonial domination of the conqueror and reaffirms their unrestricted possession as an inherent right to invasion and conquest (Barbosa, 2018a; 2021). In a colonial, patriarchal and racist order, the sentence of becoming "soulless," "faceless" and "voiceless" falls on women's bodies. According to Comandanta Miriam,

Since the arrival of the conquistadors, we have suffered the sad situation of women. They stripped us of our lands, they took away our language, our culture. This is where the domination of *caciquismo* (strongmen) enters the equation of triple exploitation, humiliation, discrimination, marginalization, mistreatment, inequality. (EZLN, 2015a, p. 109)

On the night of the armed uprising, a third of the EZLN's insurgent ranks were women, including twelve in command positions — such as captains, lieutenants, majors, and second lieutenants — leading the military occupation of the Chiapas municipalities by the indigenous army. In the hearts of these women pulsed the ancestral memory of the historical burden of the colonial, patriarchal and capitalist order, which condemned indigenous women to sexual, physical and epistemic violence and to the denial of a dignified existence. The slogan *Ya basta!* ("Enough is enough!") echoed the collective pain of that violence rooted in more than five centuries.

Other factors that boosted the political participation of Zapatista women (Barbosa, 2018a) included the high rate of indigenous infant mortality, the internal mobilization and organization of women in the communities to claim their right to political participation, and the supremacy of men under so-called legal indigenous uses and customs. Under this framework, women do not have the right to buy or inherit land; they are legally invisible. This mechanism for the reproduction of the historical denial of rights is a strategy intrinsic to the structural logic of appropriation of territories, which has as one of its main pillars the erosion of women's "traditional" rights with respect to communal land systems (Rivera Cusicanqui, 2004).

With the intensification of counterinsurgency, as an instrument of the state's ethnocidal policy, women became a strategic target, with the atrocities typical of contexts of war falling on their bodies: deprivation, executions and sexual violence (Segato, 2014). The dialectic of war in women's bodies became the core of the Zapatista women's political debate. During the First Intercontinental Meeting for Humanity and against Neoliberalism, at the Roundtable "Women and Excluded Civil Society," patriarchy was recognized as the foundation of neoliberalism and territorial expropriation promoted by transnational capital in the offensive against peoples' territories. The Zapatistas emphasized the urgency of understanding the historical roots of patriarchal oppression and of placing "gender" as a central category in the anti-capitalist struggle (EZLN, 1996).

The Revolutionary Law of Women

As already mentioned, the Revolutionary Law of Women was the first law passed by the Zapatista Autonomous Justice System, a confirmation that the Zapatista revolution was conceived, elaborated and consolidated with the central participation of women. This law is considered a normative framework for the rights and aspirations of indigenous women and the awakening of a Zapatista feminist subjectivity, which was woven into the course of community rearticulation prior to the armed insurgency, an indispensable condition in the formation of the Zapatista historical-political subject (Barbosa, 2015; 2019). It was clear to the Zapatistas that a revolutionary insurgency required, in the first place, internal political consistency and coherency in terms of equal rights. In effect, indigenous women promoted a cultural revolution, establishing that, at the community level, they would be respected as subjects of rights. According to Guadalupe, education promoter of Caracol III-Oventik:

> We within the organization, with so much lack of rights as women, saw the need to fight for equal rights between men and women .... We are talking about a revolutionary struggle, and a revolutionary struggle is not only carried out by men or only by women but is the task of everyone .... We all have a place in this struggle and that is why we must all participate in this analysis, and in the tasks that are pending. (EZLN, 2013c, p. 18)

The debate on and approval of the Revolutionary Law of Women was a pedagogical process built on the Zapatistas' "Pedagogy of the Word" in the sense of indigenous women taking the floor and making gender oppression public as an internal problem to be resolved on a priority basis (Barbosa, 2018a). In a pedagogical process, the Zapatista women debated these issues first among themselves and then in the assembly, the main space for discussion of community problems and for reaching consensus in terms of solutions. Each point of the law was raised by the women, debated and decided collectively, leading to a consensus on ten inalienable rights of women:

> In its just struggle for the liberation of our people, the EZLN incorporates women into the revolutionary struggle regardless of their race, creed, colour or political affiliation, with the only requirement of making their own the demands of exploited people and a commitment to comply with and enforce the laws and regulations of the revolution. In addition, considering the situation of all working women in Mexico, all of their just demands for equality and justice are incorporated

into the following REVOLUTIONARY LAW OF WOMEN: First: Women, regardless of race, creed, colour or political affiliation, have the right to participate in the revolutionary struggle in the place and to the degree determined by their wish and ability. Second: Women have the right to work and receive a fair wage. Third: Women have the right to decide the number of children they will have and care for. Fourth: Women have the right to participate in the affairs of the community and to hold office if they are freely and democratically elected. Fifth: Women and their children have the right to primary care for health and nutrition. Sixth: Women have the right to education. Seventh: Women have the right to choose their partner and not to be forced into marriage. Eighth: No woman may be beaten or physically abused by family members or strangers. The crimes of attempted rape or rape will be severely punished. Ninth: Women may hold leadership positions in the organization and hold military ranks in the revolutionary armed forces. Tenth: Women shall have all the rights and obligations set forth in the revolutionary laws and regulations. (Ley Revolucionaria de Mujeres 1993)

The Zapatistas began to insert the specific demands of women within the more general demands of the community, in a dialectical movement of permanence and change (Millán, 1996), that is, to overcome the patriarchy of custom and tradition. On the other hand, the Revolutionary Law of Women provokes a debate about the refoundation of the state and the nation (Millán, 2014), with the rupture of the representation of indigenous women still crystallized in the persistence of the hidden colonialism of the state. In the current context, Zapatista women continue this internal pedagogical process, including with a proposal in 1996 to expand the law with another thirty-three points, still under discussion (EZLN, 2013c). With the law, the Zapatista women began to assume civilian and military positions, at the same time deepening the collective political analysis concerning patriarchy.

In the analysis of the political documents of the Zapatista women, the following three approaches ground their conception of patriarchy as:

1. a system of oppression that is based on ethnic-racial and class divisions;

2. a way many indigenous men mimic the behaviour of the landowner; and

3. a pedagogical relationship for introducing gender domination in discussions in the communities.

In the first approach, the Zapatistas argue that the dialectic of patriarchal oppression emerges with and is articulated to the institution of private property and the dialectic of exploitation inherent in it. In the analysis by Guadalupe:

> When the institution of private property arrived, women were relegated, passed on to another level and what we call patriarchy arrived, with the dispossession of women's rights, with the dispossession of the land, it was with the arrival of private property that men began to command .... With that came the oppression by men of women for being women, and we also suffered as women at this time another discrimination for being indigenous. (EZLN, 2013c, p. 18)

The Zapatista women deepen their analysis by situating the character of patriarchal oppression, which is woven into the ethnic-racial and class dialectical nexus, in the social dynamics of the reproduction of patriarchal domination:

> Now that we are in the 21st century, there are only a few women who enjoy wealth, that is, only the women of the rich ... but in the case of us as indigenous women we continue to suffer pain, sadness, bitterness, rape, exploitation, humiliation, discrimination, imprisonment, contempt, marginalization, torture, and much more, because for us women, there is no government. (EZLN, 2015, p. 7)

Indigenous men's mimicry of the landowner is an expression of how patriarchy manifests and operates at the intersection of the public and private spheres, in terms of a sociocultural and spatial fusion in the patriarchal domination of indigenous women. In the words of Adriana, Caracol II-Oventik:

> That is why for the rest of the women of the country it remains the same, just as women lived before, as in the times of the ejidos, of the colonies, with the grandfathers dragging along the bad culture that they learned from the landowners, our grandfathers ruled the home as if they were the landowner, saying: "I am the boss," the father of the family. (p. 7)

Mariana Mora posits that the "boss-husband" constitutes the way of naming patriarchy among the Zapatistas (personal communication, 2021).[1] This can also be compared to the analysis of the so-called *entronque patriarcal,* or patriarchal convergence, that is, the confluence of the "ancestral patriar-chy" of pre-European invasion indigenous people, with the "patriarchy of the conquest," according to the theoretical analyses put forward by community feminism (Galindo, 2013). In this regard, Ana, education promoter, MAREZ El Trabajo, Caracol V, comments: "We, the indigenous peoples, incorporated into our culture the way the Spaniards treated their women; for that reason inequality between men and women began to emerge in the communities, and continues to this day" (EZLN, 2013c, p. 62).

In the sharing of the processes of political organization, the Zapatistas reveal the meaning conferred on patriarchy, linked to the identification of its pedagogical mediations, what we call here the "pedagogy of patriarchy." According to Ana,

> Such was the custom, the way of life that the Spaniards brought when they came to conquer our towns; it was the friars who educated us and instructed us in their customs and knowledge. From there we were taught that women had to serve men and always obey them when they give orders, and that women should cover their heads with a veil when they go to church, and that they should not fix their gaze anywhere, that they should keep their heads bowed. (EZLN, 2013c, p. 62)

In the view of the Zapatistas, the pedagogy of patriarchy includes two dimensions of patriarchal domination: one related to the invasion of Abya Yala (the Americas) by Europeans and responsible for establishing its bases in the structures of the state as a space of domination and power. The second patriarchal order historically interferes in the most intimate of social relations, exercising a pedagogical mediation that embeds in collective and social subjectivity on a symbolic-ideological plane the acceptance of the inferiorized place attributed to indigenous women. Therefore, this instituted social place is naturalized and all the violence inherent in it is legitimized. In this regard, Claudia, support base, MAREZ Caracol IV-Morelia, tells us:

> Women used to suffer from mistreatment and discrimination, with inequality at home and in the community. We always suffered and were told that we were a mere object, that we were good for nothing. That's how we were taught, our grandmothers only taught us to work at home, in the fields, to take care of children, animals and to serve our husbands. We never had the opportunity to go to school, so we don't know how to read or

write, let alone speak Spanish. We were told that a woman has no right to participate or to complain. We didn't know how to defend ourselves, nor did we know what a right is. This is how our grandmothers were educated by the bosses, who were the ranchers and landowners. (EZLN, 2013c, p. 46)

A palpable result of the Revolutionary Law of Women is the prohibition of alcohol consumption in Zapatista territory. As cited above, the eighth section of the law states: "No woman shall be beaten or physically abused by family members or by strangers. The crimes of attempted rape or rape will be severely punished." This section was essential to the Zapatista achievements in confronting domestic violence, which was all too often associated with the consumption of alcoholic beverages. The law makes public a process of conceptual elaboration typical of the Zapatistas, which places the ontological and epistemic bases of their social theory concerning the struggle of women in an "Epistemology of We Women" (Barbosa, 2018b). In the twenty-first century, the Zapatista women shed light on their own conception of struggle — which they call "the Struggle of Women" — which demarcates, from an epistemic and ontological matrix, the nature of the oppressions of women, especially the conception of patriarchy from the perspective of indigenous women.

Despite the low-intensity warfare in their territories, Zapatista autonomy advances and continues to develop, counting on the inclusion of women, who, little by little, are gaining spaces for political participation. Except for those who are soldiers in the EZLN itself and militiawomen in the communities, many of the rest of the Zapatista women hold positions in the autonomous governments, in the JBGs, in other areas of work in the MAREZ, as midwives, healers and traditional doctors (using herbal medicine or chiropractic) and as health promoters, education promoters, agroecology promoters, zone coordinators and *tercios compas* (media and communications specialists) (EZLN, 2013a).

To interpret the conception of feminism among Zapatista women, we need to understand the logic intrinsic to the historical forms of social organization between genders in Mesoamerican indigenous communities, which are based on the onto-epistemic matrix of complementary duality, a conceptual elaboration of nature and human beings in a duality. According to Silvia Marcos (2011), Mesoamerican duality articulates apparently contradictory discourses, demarcating a different logic with respect to the position of subjects in time and space. In the principle of complementary duality, the social roles developed by women and men in the community are recognized in a balanced way. If we return to the Revolutionary Law on Women, we clearly see the principle of complementary duality in the demand for the right to equal political participation as women.

In the theorization and experience of complementary duality, we find important concepts, such as *"lajan lajan 'aytik"* (equality and we are), "being on equal terms" or "forming together a community of equals" (Lenkersdorf, 2002). Therefore, the position of complementary peer sustains the struggle of Zapatista women for the right to equal rights to those of men, especially because of the predominance of the sexual division of labour, so present in indigenous communities, in collective work. For this reason, they refuse to build their struggle based on ideas from outside, since in their political conviction, emancipation is part of a popular political project, which must be based on a "gender paradigm" in which women and men both participate (Barbosa, 2021).

During this century, Zapatista women have organized three fundamental moments to present their political conception of the Zapatista women's struggle: the Encounter of Zapatista Women with the Women of the World, in 2007, and the First and Second International Political, Artistic, Sports and Cultural Meetings of Women Who Struggle, in 2018 and 2019. In these political events, the Zapatista women presented us with the internal process of organization of the Zapatistas, the conception of patriarchy and its oppressions, their view of struggle as "the women that we are" and their solidarity-sisterhood with the political struggle of other feminisms, especially in relation to forced disappearance and femicide.

Note

1   During the online seminar on *Feminisms, Memory and Resistance in Latin America* (2021).

Autonomy in the Construction of a Different World

In the political trajectory of Zapatismo numerous dimensions of autonomy are part of the construction of territorial self-determination and taken together constitute a strategy of struggle at the local, national and international levels. Because of lack of space in this necessarily short book, we highlight only a few of the most consolidated dimensions in the framework of autonomy; these provide an important reference for the critical social theory and political praxis of indigenous and peasant movements.

Zapatista Autonomous Justice System

The Revolutionary Law of Women, as we have seen, was the first law to structure the Zapatista Autonomous Justice System, which was made public in March 1993, nine months before the armed insurgency. The armed insurgency became necessary because of a profound historical process of social injustice in relation to the recognition of indigenous peoples as subjects of rights. The San Andrés Accords were a frame of reference in the Zapatista demands regarding what they considered a priority to be incorporated into federal, state and municipal legal systems. However, the Mexican state's non-recognition of the dialogue sessions led the Zapatistas to decide to implement the San Andrés Accords on their own, in their own territories, and to form what would become the Zapatista Autonomous Justice System.

The Zapatistas were clear that the construction and consolidation of autonomy required the formation of a legal structure that would guide the Zapatista Autonomous Government and collective work in their territories. The Zapatista Autonomous Justice System is organized into three instances of administration of justice, defined according to the degree of complexity of the matters each must address. The first instance: the authorities of the communities; the second instance: the authorities of the Zapatista rebel autonomous municipalities; and the third instance, the JBGs (Fernández Christlieb, 2014).

Likewise, the administration of the Autonomous Justice System is based on the following democratic foundations: 1. the democratic, free, direct and open election of the community authorities who would occupy the positions and remain in them in accordance with the proper performance of their functions; 2. problems must be brought to the first instance of justice, i.e. to the community authorities; 3. the most serious offences are referred to the authorities of the MAREZ; and 4. in cases where ordinary complaints are not resolved in the first and second instances of justice, an extraordinary resolution is directed within the scope of the JBG (Fernández Christlieb, 2014).

The democratic foundations of the Zapatista Autonomous Justice System result in a horizontal and close relationship physically, personally and culturally between communities and authorities, which allows access to the resolution of demands, conflicts or other problems without restrictions. The Autonomous Justice System is radically different from

Table 1. Legal Framework of the Zapatista Autonomous Justice System

Installation of Good Government	
EZLN	Instructions for Leaders and Officers of the EZLN
	War Tax Law
	Law on the Rights and Obligations of Peoples in Struggle
	Law on the Rights and Obligations of the Revolutionary Armed Forces
	Revolutionary Agrarian Law
	Revolutionary Law of Women
	Urban Reform Law
	Labour Law
	Industry and Commerce Law
	Social Security Act
	Justice Law
JBGs	Tree Care Act
	Law prohibiting the cultivation, trafficking and consumption of drugs
	Zapatista Vehicle Registration Measure
	Trafficking in Persons Act
Zapatista Communities	Public Drunkenness
	Theft
	Attempted Rape
	Drug Cultivation
	Aggravated homicide

Source: Based on Fernández Christlieb (2014)

the state justice system, which is hierarchical, bureaucratic and expensive, with extended wait times and legal language that is incomprehensible to the public. Regarding the resolution of problems and sanctions within the Autonomous Justice System, Fernández Christlieb states:

> Equally relevant to the achievement of true justice is the procedure followed for the resolution of any problem, in which the parties and their witnesses are heard, an investigation is carried out at the scene of the facts, the presence of family members is accepted, reparation of the damage is sought, and mutual agreement is sought. Work for collective benefit as a form of punishment, as well as the fact of not charging money for fines or for the service rendered, are particularities that also favor true justice. (2014, p. 219)

The Zapatista Autonomous Justice System is a permanent and popular body since the creation and approval of laws and regulations go through the community assemblies, the main democratic body of the communities. The concept of justice is inseparable from the communitarian exercise of grassroots, popular democracy, where community authorities are elected to the office on a rotating process based on the principles of commanding by obeying.

Zapatista Autonomous Rebel Education

One of the most well-known dimensions of autonomy, nationally and internationally, and a fundamental pillar of the structure of the Zapatista Autonomous Government is the political education project,[1] whose aim is to strengthen Zapatista political subjectivity (Barbosa, 2014; 2015; 2016; Baronnet, 2012; Gómez Lara, 2011; Narváez-Gutiérrez, 2005; Sáenz Boldt et. al., 2021). This educational conception is articulated in three ways: 1. the meaning of emancipatory education, which develops a critical consciousness and allows subjects to forge their political identity linked to a societal project, in the senses attributed by the tradition of popular education and the critical pedagogies of Latin America; 2. the consolidation of an education of its own — the Zapatista Autonomous Rebel Education System of National Liberation (SERAZ); and 3. Zapatismo as an educational-political movement and its pedagogical potential in teaching us philosophical, organizational and political principles, as well as a social theory and an analytical method.

SERAZ was born out of four historical-political needs: 1. to break with "official education"; 2. to construct their own schools in the MAREZ; 3. to train education promoters; and 4. to guarantee an educational process that will allow the communities to recover and strengthen the learning of the Mayan languages present in the Zapatista territories, which include Tseltal, Tzotzil, Tojolabal, Ch'ol and Zoque. Learning in their own language is considered a starting point for the educational-political work of forming children and adolescents, for which the SERAZ seeks to consolidate a curriculum whose contents are based on the culture of the Mayan indigenous peoples, as well as with the political and philosophical principles of Zapatismo (Barbosa, 2015; 2016).

The structuring of SERAZ took place gradually, at different times and in different ways in each of the first five *caracoles*. In 1995, the first initiatives were carried out in several indigenous communities in Caracol IV-Morelia. According to a collective dialogue with the Zone Education Commission and some education promoters of Caracol IV-Morelia:

> It is with enthusiasm that we began. The structure was missing. Local authorities of elders participated in the beginning, those who could read and write. Ejidal authorities began the first written words. Each municipality, Zone Commission, Municipal Commission and Delegates began to look for solidarity comrades for support in workshops (mathematics, reading-writing, politics) with the aim of having students prepared, with their own history; a history that recognizes the principle of suffering. It would be organized toward the future, with each one preparing their successor continue in the struggle .... Teachers in official government education deceive children. We are not building autonomy to steal or cheat. The importance of being autonomous is for whom and how you are going to teach. That's autonomy. We started with education clandestinely, because there was a risk of incarceration. We start with enthusiasm because education was now in our hands.

In their documents (EZLN 2013b; EZLN, n.d.) the Zapatistas share the historical process of building SERAZ in the MAREZ between 1993 and 1999, the year in which the proposal for autonomous rebel education was formalized:

> Teach the truth about our people, based on the people, that they (the people) decide what education they want; that they (the people) command .... When we decided to create Zapatista Education, it was always in consultation with the people: the teaching materials, the levels, those who would be promoters. We

consulted everywhere where there are Zapatista bases. What do you think? Everything was and is a proposal, not an imposition. We, as the Zone Education Commission, are only delegates. The people have the last word.

Initially, caravans organized by the Zapatista National Liberation Front (FZLN) (a national, peaceful civilian movement created by the Zapatistas) and international solidarity, in particular the Mexican national solidarity caravan "For Everyone, Everything," participated. The objective was to design, in dialogue with the Zapatista authorities and families, a pedagogical model that would meet the demands of education articulated within the Zapatista struggle. Another objective was to provide support in the development of didactic materials and in the first trainings of the education promoters. The Semillitas del Sol (Little Seeds of the Sun) project was one of those that contributed to these trainings. In 1998, the educational project *Ta Spol Be* began, with students who carried out their social service in Zapatista territory, for periods of six months to a year (Barbosa, 2015). The construction of the Zapatista Autonomous Rebel High School was born out of the educational project Schools for Chiapas, supported by the US non-profit organization San Diegans for Dignity, Democracy and Peace in Mexico, which provided financial and training support for promotors. In 1999, Zapatista Autonomous Education (EAZ) took its first steps in autonomous primary education with the creation of the organization New Indigenous Autonomous Education for a Just and Dignified Peace for Humanity.

With the creation of the *caracoles* in 2003, the Zapatista Movement took SERAZ completely into its own hands. School takes place over three days of classes a week and is organized into the following levels: primary: with children who do not yet know how to read and write; upper secondary school: with children who have some knowledge of literacy; and higher: with boys and girls who are proficient in reading and writing and basic mathematics skills. The curriculum includes literacy, mathematics, history, politics, nature, geography, culture, art, sports, health and agricultural production (Barbosa, 2015).

In autonomous secondary school (ESAZ), students attend classes for a period of thirty full days, including weekends, alternating with fifteen days of school break, a vacation period in which students return to their communities to share the learning acquired. ESAZ lasts three years, covering language and communication, mathematics, natural sciences, social sciences, production and humanism, where the trajectory of the

Zapatista struggle, the principles of its political project and the symbols of resistance and rebellion are reviewed. In the Zapatista Autonomous Rebel Education System, classes are held in schools and other spaces of community life, such as the *milpa*,[2] and in activities carried out in the Zapatista political struggle. In addition, learning happens collectively. According to an education promoter of Caracol III-La Garrucha, "The children are left together to do their homework so that they can move forward with each other's support." The didactic and audiovisual materials are produced in projects carried out in the *caracoles*, and all the content is decided upon in assemblies.

There is no grading system. The education promoters evaluate the participation of students in the daily dynamics of the classes. When they have learning difficulties, pedagogical alternatives are sought to help the student. According to the account of an education promoter from Caracol III-La Garrucha, "The way of teaching is based on participation. The children discussing the subject. They analyze, they express their point of view, whether or not they are doing what they are doing, and that is also coordinated with the village authorities so that everyone gets involved."

In the case of ESAZ, at the end of each cycle, the education promoters meet with the students to evaluate, collectively, what they have or have not learned. There are times when students prefer to repeat the school year because they feel they have not grasped all the content to their satisfaction. According to the principle of autonomy, SERAZ graduates do not receive any degree or certification from the Mexican government for their studies. According to the Zone Education Commission of Caracol IV-Morelia:

> We evaluate outside of the norms of the state. We work by giving students recognition: we prepare report cards for those who continue, and for those who graduate, they have a Zapatista certificate that verifies their training. The certificate may not be valid for the government, but it is worth a lot for the Zapatistas. It is undeniable, a graduate prepared to serve the people. They learn to serve the people.

Formation in Zapatista autonomous rebel education is linked to the communal perspective and co-responsibility in the educational process. It transcends the classic teacher-student relationship by calling on everyone to play a central role in their own education and political training process. Thus, families and communities are responsible for donating tortillas, beans and coffee for school food, and the education promoters do not receive any form of payment for teaching the classes. They can only work in their *milpas* on the days they are not in school, so they receive a quantity of food donated by the communities.

What role has Zapatista autonomous rebel education played in the context of the Zapatista resistance and autonomous struggle? First, it consolidates linguistic resistance. It recovers, values and strengthens the multiple meanings of the Mayan languages as a genuine expression of a way of thinking and of positioning themselves in the world, typical of the Mayan peoples of Chiapas. For example, in the Mayan world, heart and mind complement each other in community life; that is, for the Mayan peoples, thoughts, knowledge and reflections pass through the mind and through the heart, the latter being the centre of their cosmovision. That is why, for the Zapatistas, their word is *corazonada* (loosely translated as "word comes from the heart"). In the words of Subcomandante Insurgente Marcos (2007b, p. 322), "When the Zapatistas speak, we put forward the red heart that beats collectively. Understanding what we say, do and will do is impossible if our word is not felt.

The *corazonada* and *sentipensado*[3] voice that is born from this encounter between mind and heart is a bridge of dialogue that articulates a wealth of knowledge inherited from the culture, knowledge and values of ancestors and elders — that expresses a worldview in the Mayan language and is responsible for creating new horizons of meaning and subjectivities inside and outside of Zapatismo. For this reason, in the conception of autonomous rebel education, cosmovision, language and culture are central axes of the education process and have a strategic role in the struggle for autonomy, since many words of the Mayan languages allow us to think about the world in a different way from those that have only Spanish as a reference (Barbosa, 2014; 2015; 2016).

The education promoters emphasize that learning Castilla[4] is a fundamental strategic element in linguistic resistance, as it allows them to link up with the Kaxlan (mestizo) world, avoid marginalization and abuse and "be able to defend themselves." This educational need was strengthened, above all, after the Acteal Massacre.[5] The affected communities were fully aware that not being fluent in Spanish represented a great political and legal limitation, mainly to demand, before the relevant legal entities, the trial and punishment of those responsible for the massacre. At the same time, SERAZ allows a pedagogical refoundation of territory and community, giving new meaning to educational practice, with the strengthening of experience and knowledge.

The principle of community life, typical of indigenous communities, expresses a different way of understanding time and space that is reflected in education times and spaces. Although the school is a central space, the daily practice of education and learning also takes place in other settings: the family, the community (in the context of the assemblies, the *caracoles*, and the JBGs) and the *milpa*, following the rhythms of time in the community, that is, of sowing, harvesting and political activities. The "geopedagogy" of Zapatista knowledge (Barbosa, 2015; 2016) is a relationship that is established between school and community life by incorporating the set of knowledge that is born from the daily life of indigenous communities in their own territory and through their own cultural legacy. And community life, as an educational principle, is the collective learning of autonomy, expressed in participation in the assembly, in collective work, and in the JBG. The Zapatista pedagogy accompanies the movement of struggle and resistance where learning is born and develops from experience, knowledge and, above all, the successes, limits and possibilities that flow from their collective action. Also called "a pedagogy of feeling-thinking and feeling-knowing" (Barbosa, 2014), which is built on the idea of *corazonada* — a *sentipensado* pedagogy, which weaves the word, the silence and the political action of Zapatismo and its struggle for autonomy.

Another central aspect of SERAZ is the result of the implementation of the Revolutionary Law of Women in the MAREZ. Point six of the law (women have the right to education) was fundamental in strengthening the educational and political formation of the Zapatistas. Spanish is the language that mediates the institutional discourse of the state, under the yoke of patriarchy, that hegemonically defines the conception of justice and rights from the perspective of white privilege, a historical construction inherent to the colonial project in Latin America, and that transcends it by reproducing it in the norms of constitutional law of the modern nation-state and its capacity to veto the rights of indigenous populations, in particular indigenous women.

By accessing educational training, one opens the way to an understanding of legal codes and their ambiguities, while questioning the epistemological authority of the state and modern Western rationality. With the learning of Spanish, the Zapatista women disputed the language of legal proceedings when they laid the foundations of Zapatista Autonomous Justice, with the first law in force in their territories — built collectively by the women, in their mother tongues, though finally written in Spanish, to demarcate their position as subjects as well as their epistemic autonomy. They are pioneers in the development of a legal framework to confront the patriarchal convergence (Galindo, 2013) with a law that little by little has become a reference document for the struggle of women in Mexico and in the world.

Another dimension that we highlight in the educational conception of Zapatismo has to do with the reverberations — in other spaces outside the autonomous territories — of the set of learnings acquired in the experience of Zapatista autonomous struggle. Saénz Boldt, et al. (2021) have named this "Pedagogy of the Zapatista Seed," in that others, in other places, learn from and are inspired by the Zapatista struggle:

> As a process of broad self-reflexive construction that takes place across time and space, forming a collective revolutionary subjectivity in diverse geographies both inside and outside the autonomous communities. This exogenous collective subjectivity, in the case of the Pedagogy of the Zapatista Seed, is woven from various encounters of people, collectives and social movements with Zapatismo. (Saénz Boldt, et al., 2021, p. 4)

In other words, the Zapatistas continue to transgress the boundaries of teaching-learning through a series of activities convened and organized by them, in which hundreds of people from different countries of the world, as well as in Mexico, participate. These spaces have an educational-pedagogical potential with respect to apprehending Zapatista political theory, the principles of commanding by obeying and, above all, the hope of uniting the struggles in a collective educational and political process. In dialogue with the legacy of Paulo Freire (1987), we would say that it is the construction of a "pedagogy of the oppressed" for the critical analysis of contemporary forms of domination, exploitation and power, but also articulated to an emancipatory horizon of thought that is constructed collectively.

Zapatista Economy

Zapatista autonomy and self-government are almost entirely self-financed through various mechanisms. One is with the collection of taxes on the sales of products of the cooperatives, for example, coffee, outside the Zapatista territory and the country. But it is the "collective works" that finance most of the autonomous public services in the communities. Families give hours of work to the collective work that involves them. There are collective works to maintain each autonomous school, with its education promoters, each autonomous clinic, with its health promoters, each autonomous pharmacy, each autonomous store, the expenses of each MAREZ, each *caracol*, and so on, as well as the Zapatista army. Collective herds of cattle in each community represent a "collective accumulation." When the authorities and the assembly decide by consensus in favour of some community investment, they can sell one or more cows to cover the cost. In the same way, the herd functions as "collective insurance" for the community. When a family's house is destroyed by a fire, the assembly decides to sell cows for reconstruction. Or when someone gets sick or has an accident and has a condition so serious that the autonomous health system (which even has regional hospitals) cannot resolve it, the person is taken to the city in an autonomous ambulance, and one or more cows are sold to pay for the treatments.

The support that the Zapatistas receive from national and international solidarity movements and from European cooperation agencies (typically Basque and Italian), in their totality adds up to a small fraction of the budgets that the official non-Zapatista municipalities get from the Mexican government, which the autonomous municipalities do not receive and do not want to receive.

With respect to the Zapatista economy, beyond the presuppositions of autonomy and collective insurance, there are both the agricultural production plots of each family and the collective work of groups or individuals and families. They can be growing vegetables, coffee or flowers, raising animals, making handicrafts, boots and shoes, or baking bread or making tortillas; there are even autonomous car repair garages. Those who produce certain items, such as coffee or pigs, are organized into cooperatives and producer associations.

A central emphasis of the autonomous economy is to recover the local economy of the rural village and the territory that surrounds it, which was lost in the era of globalization and the exodus from the countryside. In Zapatismo, each community must have families producing various foods as well as autonomous collective stores — managed by rotating collectives — which buy wholesale in the city what is not produced locally and resell at cost to Zapatista consumers. Each village should have its bakery, tortilla shop, seamstress, tailor, shoemaker, mechanic, musical groups and so on. At the Fray Bartolomé de Las Casas Indigenous Centre for Integral Training– University of the Land (CIDECI-Unitierra) in San Cristóbal de las Casas, the youth of the communities come to study and learn the trades that are needed in their community, with the idea of returning and setting up their small business for the reconstruction of the local economy. The owners of means of transportation (vans, minivans, etc.) are organized into Zapatista transport cooperatives and societies that offer transportation services for both people and products throughout the Zapatista territory. The *caracoles* are grouped into large zones, which have two large trucks that constantly move between them, facilitating what might be called an "inter-zone trade," for example, where the lowland, tropical climate territories exchange their products with the temperate territories of the highlands.

The Zapatista economy incorporates discussions in the village assemblies regarding the causes and effects of soil erosion and environmental degradation, such as the uncontrolled felling of trees and the use of agrochemicals and transgenic seeds in crops. Likewise, they incorporate the Zapatista strategy for the creation of ecological and agroecological environmental alternatives, such as the use of organic fertilizers and natural pesticides for the efficient control of flora and fauna pests, water conservation, soil management and beehive care, among others (Martínez Cuero, 2022; Val and Rosset, 2022). The following excerpt from a special broadcast of Radio Insurgente, *The Voice of the Voiceless*, on August 25, 2007, reflects on the importance of land and Mother Earth for the Zapatista communities:

> This is the voice of the voiceless, the voice of the Zapatista Army of National Liberation. We started the news about Mother Earth by talking about how capitalism exploits her and how it does not take care of her or respect her. It is therefore capital that does not care that our Mother Earth is angry with us, they only care about money.... We, as indigenous people and peasants, must take care of the land because it is the basis for life and the construction of our autonomy. We, the indigenous Zapatistas, because we Zapatistas must take care of the forests, the rivers, and continue to collectively respect them .... We take care of our rivers, lakes, mountains, and everything. For us, the Zapatista peoples, the earth is not only our Mother Earth but it is also our life, and in it we live and we die. That is why it is forbidden to cut down trees on the banks of rivers, because it damages our natural resources. (Martínez Cuero, 2013, p. 139)

In general, the standard of living of Zapatista families and communities is higher than that of non-Zapatista communities, as evidenced by the comparative plethora of Zapatista cattle and pickup trucks and the construction of their houses with higher quality materials. It has also been widely observed over the years that the Zapatista families have increased their food production, while that of the other families has decreased significantly, an effect that can be attributed to the greater out-migration of non-Zapatista families and to their incorporation into government social programs that give them direct cash transfers, which have encouraged them to abandon food production for their consumption and to buy their food in the market. Among the ironies we have witnessed is that many non-Zapatista families buy food from Zapatista families and that the construction materials the Mexican government often gives free of charge to non-Zapatista families (as part of the counterinsurgency) are sold by the "beneficiaries" of government largesse to Zapatista families, because in many cases the former are only saving money in order to be able to migrate to the city or to the United States, while the Zapatistas are committed to staying in their communities and thus invest in their homes.

The Zapatista economy is based on collective accumulation, while the non-Zapatista economy is based on individual accumulation. However, individual accumulation is often not "real" accumulation, since even though the money from government social programs flows to the non-Zapatista family bank account in fairly large quantities, it goes out even faster, in the consumption of alcohol and other drugs (prohibited under Zapatismo), in the increased prices of basic foodstuffs and medicines, in frivolous consumption, and in all the other "evils" that accompany the insertion of the poor into the capitalist economy. Meanwhile, collective accumulation provides a great capacity to mobilize. For example, the massive 2012 March of Silence when thousands of Zapatistas marched silently through various cities in Chiapas,[6] was made possible by the hundreds of vans of the Zapatista transport societies and cooperatives, which not only brought people to the city for the march but also sacks of food from the autonomous collective warehouses.

Finally, for Zapatismo, to the extent possible, *everything* must be autonomous. In food production, this has meant the promotion of processes to promote agroecology instead of production dependent on chemical inputs from outside, which creates dependence rather than autonomy (Rosset and Altieri, 2017). Food production is not autonomous if it depends on external inputs (Rosset and Martínez Torres, 2016). One of the authors of this book has participated in several Zapatista agroecology meetings in two *caracoles* and has on numerous occasions interviewed a now retired Zapatista agroecology coordinator. At the time of an interview conducted a few years ago, one of the *caracoles* had more than 220 agroecology promoters, five agroecology training centres and a laboratory for the local production of bio-inputs, above all for coffee production. In a meeting with the promoters of another *caracol*, a video was shown about agroecology in Cuba, an example recognized worldwide for the success of the promotion of agroecology "from peasant to peasant" (Machín Sosa et al., 2010). In the discussion after the video, a Zapatista coordinator commented: "This video has been shown in many Zapatista communities, and our people love it" because "Cuba is the example of an entire autonomous country," and because of that, they are inspired by its agroecological example.

In conclusion, the reconstruction of an autonomous, or at least semi-autonomous, peasant and rural local economy, based on collective accumulation, is emblematic of what we pointed out above: the coherence between theory, discourse and praxis represents one of the great achievements and lessons learned from Zapatismo.

Notes

1 We use the word "project "not to refer to something funded by a grant, but rather to a "political project."

2 *Milpa* refers both to the traditional Mesoamerican farming system based on maize, beans, and squash in rotation with managed forest regeneration and to the actual physical space or plot where the mixture of corn, beans, and other useful plants species are cultivated.

3 While *sentipensado* could be loosely translated as "heartfelt," the Latin American noun, *sentipensamiento* ("feeling-thinking"), refers to a much deeper notion of thought that not only comes from the rational, Cartesian mind, but that also comes from our feelings, so that ideas are simultaneously thought and felt, as in the concept of the *corazonada* word.

4 "Castilla" is the way the Zapatistas refer to Spanish, instead of *Español* or *Castellano*.

5 The Acteal Massacre was a paramilitary attack on the community of Acteal, in the municipality of Chenalhó, Chiapas, on December 22, 1997, with the murder of forty-five people, including children and pregnant women. The community was holding a vigil for peace when they were attacked and slaughtered.

6 See https://www.elsaltodiario.com/hemeroteca-diagonal/la-marcha-zapatista-mas-grande-de-la-historia-del-ezln for further details.

Zapatista Critical Theory

> The goal of critical thinking is not to find the truth (and therefore build a new alibi for the arbitrariness of the moment), but to question "truths," confront them, dismantle them and show them as what they are.... Critical thinking is not just a theoretical position. It is, above all, an ethical position in relation to knowledge and reality. (EZLN, 2024x)

From armed insurgency to popular, or peoples', and class-based autonomy, the Zapatista Movement has promoted a true educational and pedagogical process inside and outside its autonomous territories. The conformation of the Zapatista historical-political subject is the result of this educational and political formation, in which a paradigm of alternative and revolutionary thought is vindicated, and of an inseparable link between cosmovision, culture, ancestral knowledge, territory and a political praxis that is a constitutive part of its history. In the words of the Zapatistas, the role of autonomous rebel education is:

> To value knowledge as a path toward development and preserving culture based on the historical and cultural roots of peoples. To value the educational process not only as the set of knowledge itself, but also as the specific tools of each group for its application. To promote the interaction of cultures, which will allow their mutual enrichment. To recover and value traditional knowledge to restimulate the identity of peoples and individuals. To promote education in the mother tongue in addition to the language used as a vehicle for interaction. To respect the right of each culture to decide autonomously on their educational process, both in terms of methods and of content, as well as in terms of human and material resources. (EZLN, 1996, p. 124–125)

In their political trajectory, the Zapatista Movement has developed a critical social and political theory and a method of anti-capitalist, anti-colonial and anti-patriarchal analysis, which can be seen in their documents, communiqués and political events, such as the Zapatista School[1] and the

International Seminar on Critical Thinking in the Face of the Capitalist Hydra,[2] both with publications that condense central elements of Zapatista social and political theory and praxis. From there emerges a "theory of the jungle," according to González Casanova (1997), which is to problematize and theorize political theory from another place. It is a process of conceptual elaboration inseparable from the concrete reality of what the Capitalist Hydra represents in the face of the anti-systemic and anti-capitalist struggles of our historical time.

Zapatista social and political theory comes from a rigorous method of analysis based on their own existence as peoples and on the identification of the problems they have faced, which make up the contradictions inherent in the historical process of colonialism and capitalism. They have developed a theoretical work that allows us to access an explanatory horizon of such problems, not restricted to an analytical approach of what is experienced in a localized way, as territories located in a specific region of Mexico, but rather emphasizing that they are problems of historical scale that are dialectically linked to experience at the local scale. Capitalism, patriarchy, imperialism and colonialism are phenomena of global magnitude. The original character of the cultural and political experience of Zapatismo means that Zapatista social and political theory has a great creative capacity to elaborate its own explanatory categories to think about ourselves dialectically, linked to global processes.

Zapatismo has shaped and instigated, in dialogue with a series of intellectuals, a theoretical and methodological development for the critical approach to new (or not before seen as a priority) and old social problems. We highlight those that seem to us to be the most significant in the foundation of Zapatista autonomy, and that are related to 1. the indigenous as a political category in social class theory; 2. the theory of the state, power and capitalism; and 3. the theory of praxis and peoples and class autonomy.

The Indigenous as a Political Category in a Theory of Class

One framework in Zapatista social and political theory is the relocation of the "indigenous," moving from a purely ethnic take to the *indigenous as a historical-political subject,* placing the indigenous question at the centre of contemporary theoretical and political debate, as not only a national but also a regional and global issue.[3] The choice of January 1, 1994, for the armed insurgency was no coincidence: it was the start date the North American Free Trade Agreement (NAFTA), a trilateral agreement that would allow free access to water and mineral resources in Mexican territory by US and Canadian transnationals. The state of Chiapas was one of the most strategic for the advance of capitalism by plunder, or accumulation by dispossession, in the entire Mesoamerican region. With the unexpected insurgency of an indigenous army, Chiapas became emblematic of the reconfiguration of capitalism in the Global South, making this Mexican state the starting point in the advance and consolidation of this new stage of capitalism.

Although many Zapatista documents and communiqués denounce the historical social and political exclusion of indigenous peoples, the underlying demand was not limited to ethnic recognition by the Mexican state. On the contrary, from the San Andrés Accords to the declaration of radical autonomy, the Zapatistas demanded the recognition by the state of their *political and territorial* existence. This represented a key political positioning — demarcating the territories of interest to financial and transnational capitalism as not *empty land,* as governments and colonizers have always called the lands of indigenous peoples. They are territories inhabited since before the long night of 500 years by the millenary existence of "original peoples" with an ontological and epistemic way of inhabiting and caring for these territories. And they clearly situate these peoples not so much in merely ethnic terms, but in terms of class, of "those from below," in Zapatista words, and "rebels" vis-à-vis the Western state:

> By "original peoples" we mean not only the mis-named "indigenous" but all the peoples who originally looked after the territories that today face wars of conquest, such as the Kurdish people, and who are subsumed, by force, by the so-called Nation States. (EZLN, 2018a)[4]

In a greeting to the Fifth Congress of the Landless Workers Movement (MST) in Brazil, the Zapatistas elaborated:

> With you we have seen and suffered the war of conquest, and we are not referring to those carried out five hundred years ago by the Portuguese and Spanish monarchies, but to those carried out today by the empires of money. They, those above, expel us from the land, imposing their models of cultivation that are not ours. They poison the land with their transgenic seeds and exploit those who work the land under conditions of slavery, while at the same time throwing millions of people into the slow death of unemployment, strengthening the *latifundia* (large landholding estates), which, as in colonial times, humiliate the land, those who work it and those who live on it. We know, as you do, that this is not only happening in Brazil and in our Mexico, but that it takes

place in all the great bleeding wound that is our Latin America and throughout the world. Capitalism has adopted its most brutal and murderous face, that of wars with bullets and bombs, and that of wars with laws and authorities. (Carrano, 2007)

From an analysis of the national question related to Chiapas, two fundamental issues emerge for a comprehensive critical interpretation: 1. as an essential condition for its expanded reproduction, the development of capitalism on a global scale requires deepening the expropriation of land and territory in the Global South, in national and regional contexts; 2. class struggle in the Global South is not limited to the terms of classical Marxism, of the antagonism between the proletariat (industrial workers) and the bourgeoisie (factory owners), but rather between "those above" and "those below" (something like the 99% versus the 1%). Nor is it limited to an identity-based approach, of recognition of "indigenous peoples" in a multicultural perspective. The territories of interest of capitalism by plunder are inhabited by a diversity of peoples, not only indigenous, but also peasants, traditional communities and fishers, among many others who are driven from their way of existence by the advance of land and territory grabbing. The denunciation of capitalism by plunder and the defence of territorial autonomy in Zapatista political praxis, we argue, allows us to understand an approach that transcends the ethnic question, moving to the *question of class and peoples*. It also dialogues with the work of Peruvian scholar José Carlos Mariátegui and with the concept, in African thought, of "working people," which encompasses both formal and informal workers, such as street vendors, rural workers, peasants and so on (Shivji, 2017).

In 2007, during the Second Meeting of the Zapatista Peoples with the Peoples of the World, the Zapatistas deepened this analysis, in a Marxian perspective, by emphasizing that the defence of the land constitutes the key strategy to challenge capitalism and move forward along the path of human emancipation. In the words of Lieutenant Colonel Insurgente Moisés:

The land where the comrades are now is their property, we recovered it. We discovered that, to destroy the capitalists, we have to become the owners of where we work, because that's how capitalism functions. You work on farms or in factories, and the profit is not for the working people. In our practice we are more interested in how to attack the capitalist system, as you will see during these days of this second meeting of the Zapatista peoples with the peoples of the world. They will have a lot to tell you about the experiences of their comrades, because now the means of production, *the land*, is in their hands. It is the fundamental basis of their lives. It is also understood that land is the basis for capitalists to exploit, as the means of production. The *compañeros* and *compañeras* of the Zapatista peoples, when they seized this means of production, that is, the land, began to work it communally, locally, regionally, municipally, that is, in collectives, production societies, cooperatives. This has been achieved, thanks to the recovery of, the taking back of, the land; without that, we would not be where we are now. It is clear to us, the Zapatistas, that when we became the owners of these lands, as the owners of the means of production, it was and is our main way to attack capitalism, though we still have a lot to do. But we already know where we want to go. We realized all this when we took back the land of the so-called bosses, the landowners or *latifundistas*. We chased them away, with our struggle of January 1, 1994, the history that you already know. (EZLN, 2007a, s/p)

From a Zapatista perspective, there is a way of being, of living, that is an indigenous political sociability with deep territorial roots. Territory is understood as the historical experience of the existence of peoples with history, with culture and in coexistence with other beings, as we can observe in the words of Comandanta Keli: "For indigenous, peasant and rural peoples, land and territory are more than just sources of work and food; they are also culture, community, history, ancestors, dreams, future, life and mother" (Rosset, 2007, p. 160). Similarly, for Comandante Tacho:

> Indigenous peoples and peasants have historically had our roots in these territories; we relate to them through Mother Earth. There we produce our food to live, there we were born, there we develop, in it we multiply and coexist, with the mountains, with the rivers, with the air, with the life of nature itself, the seas, the springs, as well as in it live all living beings with the right to life, as well as the resources of the subsoil. We, the indigenous, peasants, take care of and love our Mother Earth, and we have demonstrated this for centuries. (Rosset, 2007, p. 159)

In Mexico's recent history, the Zapatistas have been a fundamental voice in the permanent denunciation of this predatory model of capitalism by dispossession and plunder, which continues its course in contemporary Mexico with the megaprojects of the Maya Train and the Trans-Isthmus Corridor, widely denounced by the National Indigenous Congress (CNI) and the EZLN (CNI, 2019; EZLN, 2020; *La Jornada*, 2020).

Zapatista Theory of the State, Power and Capitalism

Although some scholars interpret the social and political theory of Zapatismo as a rupture with Marxism, we argue that in it there is a theory of the state, power and capitalism very much in line with the terms analyzed in Marxian theory,[5] distinguishing itself in the rupture with vanguardism and electoral parties and in the emancipatory horizon articulated by autonomy.

At the International Seminar on Critical Thinking in the Face of the Capitalist Hydra, the Zapatistas deepened their analysis of the different dimensions of capitalism by plunder, to elucidate, from the perspective of political economy, its different stages and impacts on indigenous and peasant territories. By alluding to the Greek mythology of the Lernaean Hydra to refer to the many heads of capitalism, they evoke the challenges posed to all the struggles present in Latin American rural areas to confront an economic model increasingly rooted in transnational capital and in a legal framework that institutionalizes and legitimizes the process of territorial expropriation and predatory capitalist extractivism. In the first volume of the book that was produced from the seminar (EZLN, 2015a), we can see the elaboration of a theory of the state and power. The same is true of the series of Zapatista communiqués entitled "300" (EZLN, 2018a; 2018b; 2018c), which dialogue with the theory of dependence, especially when identifying the dependent and subordinate integration of peripheral countries into globalized capitalism, with particular attention to so-called "progressive" presidents, who in practice do not break with these structures. On this point the dialectical method of analysis is precise:

> We start by analyzing what is happening in the world, then we go down to what is happening on the continent, then we go down to what is happening in the nation, then in the region and then locally. And from there we began to go back up from the local to the regional, the national, the continental and to the worldwide. (EZLN, 2018a)

In this theory, the historical role of the state as administrator of imperialist and capitalist politics in national contexts is highlighted, functioning as an instance of legitimation of the legal and military apparatus that guarantees the mechanisms for the full reproduction of capital. A central argument of the seminar (EZLN, 2015a) was the reaffirmation that the genealogy of the Capitalist Hydra is based on war as a strategy for capitalism to maintain, historically, its ideological and political-economic hegemony. This can be either in national contexts, violently imposing new patterns of capital accumulation, such as concessions to mining companies, wind farms or other mega-projects, with the dispossessions, displacements, disappearances and murders in indigenous and peasant territories; or even in international geopolitics, in the constant wars driven by imperialist policy, especially in the Middle East.

Likewise, during the same seminar, the Zapatistas warned about the great mistake, common among the progressive left, of confusing "government" with "power": "perhaps they should study a little and learn that to be in government is not to have power" (EZLN, 2015a, p. 348). The question of the (non-)seizure of power was a fertile debate in the years of the Soviet Revolution, finding in the voice and pen of Rosa Luxemburg nodal questions about the very course of the revolutionary process. "Reform or revolution?" was the concern that pulsed in Luxemburg's political reflections and that instigated an enormous variety of writings on the process of building social-ism. The same concern pulsated throughout the International Seminar on Critical Thinking in the Face of the Capitalist Hydra.

In the emblematic communiqué "300, Part One: A Hacienda, One World, One War, Few Probabilities" (EZLN, 2018a), Zapatista social and political theory sheds light on the dynamics of the structures of domination and power of an imperialist and neocolonial capitalism in its international face and in national contexts. At the national level, the "state form" pre-serves its capitalist nature and subordinate, dependent integration into the global economy. States will have different kinds of governments at different times, according this analysis. But whether it is a "progressive democracy" that contains dissent through class conciliation, or an "autocratic dicta-torship" that represses dissent, will depend on what capitalism needs at a given moment. Making use of a metatheoretical language, Zapatismo resorts to the metaphor of the "world as a hacienda," with a "good *capataz,* or foreman," or a "bad foreman" to explain, in a peasant language, how the imperialist and neocolonial character of capitalism operates and the role played by the national government in peripheral economic contexts, as is the case not only in Mexico but also in the context of the capitalist system in Latin America, Africa and Asia. In these words, they analyze the imperialist dynamics of capitalism:

> So that's how we saw it, and it continues. We think that's how capitalism is now. It wants to turn the world into a hacienda. The owner of a transnational corporation can say: "I'm going to my hacienda in Mexico," or depending on what he wants: "I'm going to my hacienda in Guatemala, or in Honduras" and so on. (EZLN, 2018a)

In Zapatista social and political theory, the permanent reconfiguration of capitalism obeys patterns of exploitation, domination and power that are constitutive of its historical nature: the violent expropriation of territories; the overexploitation of the labour force; the commodification of nature for the maximization of profits; the search for new markets; the enhancement of consumerism; successive wars; the imposition of capitalist rationality as a civilizational paradigm; and the deepening of exclusion and misery.

The capitalist system is advancing in the way it conquers territories, destroying as much as it can …. The system is advancing in its reconquest of the world. It doesn't matter what is destroyed, what is left or what is left over: everything is disposable if you make the maximum profit as quickly as possible. The capitalist machine is returning to the methods that gave rise to it — which is why we recommend reading the original Accumulation of Capital — that it is through violence and war that new territories are conquered. It is as if capitalism left a part of the conquest of the world pending in neoliberalism, and now it must complete it. In its development, the system "discovers" that new commodities have appeared, and those new commodities are in the territory of the indigenous peoples: water, land, air, biodiversity. Everything that is not yet corrupted is in the territory of the indigenous peoples and they are coming for it all. When the system seeks (and conquers) new markets, they are not only markets for consumption, for buying and selling goods; also, and above all, it seeks and tries to conquer territories and populations to extract everything it can from them, no matter that, at the end, it leaves a wasteland as a legacy and evidence of its passage …. The "development" and "progress" offered by the system hide the fact that it is their own development and progress, and, most importantly, it conceals the fact that such development and progress come at the cost of death and the destruction of populations and territories …. To civilize an indigenous community is to convert its population into a salaried labour force, that is, with the capacity to consume. That is why all the programs of the state are aimed at "the incorporation of the marginalized population into civilization." And, as a result, the indigenous peoples would no longer demand respect for their ways of life but rather would demand "help" to "place their products on the market" and "to obtain employment." In short: the optimization of poverty. (EZLN, 2018a)

The critique of the political limits of governments is based on a fundamental Marxian premise: in a capitalist society, the state is an institution that administrates the structures of capital, and governments are elected to play a regulatory role in the dynamics of the functioning of the capitalist system. Zapatismo explains it with the analogy of a mega-hacienda (the world), with an owner (capital), where the countries are the individual haciendas that make up the global mega-hacienda. The presidents of the hacienda-countries are the foremen, good or bad, who manage each hacienda for the owner, ensuring the full functioning of a dependent and peripheral economic polity.

Obviously, there is a hegemonic dispute in Gramscian terms. However, in a capitalist society, the state is capitalist, the political and economic forces hold class hegemony and the political leadership of the capitalist development model, and overcoming it requires a revolutionary process. Hence the provocative critique of the Zapatistas: "Will they be satisfied with a change of foreman or boss, or do they want freedom?" (EZLN, 2018a). In other words, "What does freedom mean for the Zapatistas?" Are you satisfied with removing the bad foreman and replacing them with a good foreman? And they say, we, the Zapatistas, don't want to have any foremen.

By pointing out the fallacy of bourgeois democracy and the persistence of a capitalist state under progressive governments, the Zapatistas demonstrate the imminent risk of assuming a position in government, which would break the synchronicity between the necessary preparation of forces for a revolutionary process and the construction of a true people's hegemony. Therefore, they reinvigorate the possibilities of emancipatory struggle through revolution, even if it is the revolution of autonomy, something that must be valued in the face of a political moment in which capitalism celebrates the "death" of socialism as a political project. When they take up arms, they do so inspired by the revolutionary legacy, a demonstration that revolution is the work of the oppressed of the world, a condition that is not limited to the urban proletariat (Barbosa, 2017).

More recently, the Zapatistas used the Israeli war on Gaza and the way in which organized crime operates in Mexico and other countries to explain how the state, whether led by right-wing politicians or by so-called progressives, and organized crime both essentially work in the same marketplace, serving the interests of capital:

> There is no difference between progressive and right-wing politicians, just as there are no fundamental differences between good and bad bosses. Both manage dispossession .... At its current

stage, the system is waging a new war of conquest, and its goal is to destroy/rebuild, depopulate/repopulate. Destruction/ depopulation and reconstruction/reordering of an area is the fate of that war. The Israeli government is not avenging the Hamas attacks of October 7, 2023; it is destroying and de- populating a territory. The business is not only in destruction and mass murder; it will be in reconstruction and reordering. That is why there is an obvious complicity among the nation-states of the world. When nations send military supplies to Israel, they are not only supporting the genocide against the Palestinian people. They are investing in that crime. The dividends from that business will come later ... [just as] so-called megaprojects do not lead to development. They are only commercial corridors opened so that organized crime has new markets. The dispute between rival cartels is not only about human and drug traffick- ing; it's above all the dispute over the monopoly of the floor fee in what is wrongly called the "Maya Train" and the "Trans-Isthmus Corridor" [megaprojects to build transit corridors for capital]. Trees and animals cannot be charged fees, but communities and companies that settle on that other useless border in the southeast of Mexico can. This ensures the growth of wars for territorial control, in which the hologram of the nation-state will be absent. Starting from the criterion that the violence of what they call "organized crime" is an anomaly of the system is not only false, but it also prevents us from understanding what is happening (and from acting accordingly). It is not an irregularity but a consequence. The objective is consensual: the state wants an open market ("free" of intruders — that is, of indigenous peoples), and the others want control of a territory .... Those who say that there is an alliance between governments and organized crime are lying. Just as there is no alliance between a company and its clients. What there is, is a simple — albeit costly — commercial operation: the state offers an absence and the cartel in question "buys" that absence and replaces the presence of the state in a town, region, zone, country. The gain is mutual between seller and buyer, the loss is for those who survive in those places. "Whoever pays or lends, commands" is the old aphorism that analysts and "social scientists" "forget." (EZLN, 2024)

The absence of the state in many areas of Mexico (and other Latin American countries) gives "organized crime" a free reign to extort protection payments (floor fees) from families and local businesses, while terrorizing them through a reign of violence. The end result is the same as in Gaza: people eventually flee and territories are depopulated, which is the starting point for their re-purposing by capital to profit from reconstruction, agribusiness, mining and other enterprises. Thus do both the state and organized crime serve capital, according to the Zapatistas, without any need for direct collusion between them.

Zapatista Theory of Praxis, and Peoples', Popular and Class Autonomy

Another fundamental contribution of Zapatista social and political theory is the centrality of *praxis* as a core element of a revolutionary theory and of the project of autonomy itself. In the case of Zapatismo, praxis leads to Freire's pedagogical principle of reflection-action-reflection, what the Zapatistas call *caminar preguntando* (walking while asking questions). This is clear in the sense of autonomy as coherence between theory and practice:

> Neither theory without practice, nor practice without theory, we have said .... What we are pointing out is that those who do theory must do practice — we would almost say by scientific method .... And those who do practice must reflect on it, not only because, if they depend on a theorist to explain and direct them, they will end up with... How can I break the news to them? Well, they will end up being anxious about whether to vote or not; also, and above all, because we must remember that our struggle does not have a defined time limit but, rather, encompasses entire generations. (EZLN, 2015, p. 213–214)

The Zapatista autonomic project incorporates a popular, or peoples', or class dimension, a political identity common to the tradition of Latin American and Caribbean popular struggles. In documents and communiqués, we can identify the category "people" as the *ethos* of the Zapatista historical-political subject, that is, that the process of liberation and emancipation must be assumed as a popular political commitment "because only the people are going to liberate themselves; no one is going to give them their freedom, not a leader, not a man or a woman, is going to give them freedom" (EZLN, 2015a, p. 36). "The solutions are made by the people themselves, not by leaders, and not by partisans" (p. 343). The character of popular, or peoples', autonomy, refers to a horizontality in the Zapatista political work, reflected in the seven principles of commanding by obeying, which were listed earlier.

The theory of Zapatista praxis incorporates an ontological and epistemic matrix of political philosophy and the categories that emerge from Mayan languages (Barbosa, 2015; 2016). Language serves as an entry into the world and culture of indigenous peoples, capturing the meanings and symbologies that express their ways of reading the world and belonging to the world (Lenkersdorf, 2005). The sense of intersubjectivity in the indigenous cultural and linguistic structure transcends all the areas and spaces in which their cosmovision is manifested, in which the inseparable link between language and lived reality is demonstrated. In comparison to so-called "modern language," indigenous language embodies real life experience of people living with Mother Earth. This reveals how indigenous peoples weave interpretive views and meanings about the world and themselves in interaction with the world. In this way of seeing the world lies the process of shaping a political intersubjectivity and a social and collective identity as peoples (Barbosa, 2015). In the categorical framework of Zapatismo, we highlight some concepts[6] that are central to Zapatista political praxis, such as *tik* (something like "we") and *mandar'ay* (control). According to Carlos Lenkersdorf, *tik*

> emphasizes a group identity and not an individual one .... In the group exchange of ideas, each of the participants speaks of the *we* and not the *I*. Obviously, each of the participants knows and respects that relationship that we call *nosotric* (something akin to "we-ness") and that orients everyone towards an agreement, instead of each one speaking for himself, convinced of his ideas to pull the others in his direction. (2002, p. 32)

From the *nosotric*, or "we" action — evident in the Zapatista slogan "*Detrás de nosotros estamos ustedes*" (something like "behind *us*, are *we* who are *you*") — derives a form of socio-political organization and an intersubjectivity that conforms to certain principles of community sociability, which situates the social place of each member of the community — children, men, women, the elderly — while demarcating a certain view of the social reality internal and external to the communities, closely related to the organizational principle of territories (Barbosa, 2015). Likewise, *tik* incorporates a sense of popular otherness, in the sense of recognition of the other not as someone inferior, who must be educated to accept a single form of reasoning, a single form of thought, which leads to a symbolic and ideological

domination that subjugates certain social and productive relations proper
to capital. According to Subcomandante Insurgente Marcos:

> Our strength, if we have any, is in this recognition: we are who
> we are, and there are others who are who they are, and there is
> another for whom we do not yet have the word to name, yet they
> are who they are. When we say "we," we are not absorbing, and
> thus subordinating, identities, but highlighting the bridges that
> exist between different pains and different rebellions. We are the
> same because we are different. In the Sixth [Declaration of the
> Lacandón Jungle], the Zapatistas reiterate our rejection of any
> attempt at hegemony, that is, of any vanguardism, whether it
> touches us at the front or aligns us, as throughout these centuries,
> in the rearguard .... We know that the boss cannot be defeated by
> a single thought, a single force, a single directive (no matter how
> revolutionary, consistent, radical, ingenious, numerous, powerful
> and other things that directive may be). It is the teaching of our
> dead that diversity and difference are not weaknesses for the
> underworld, but the strength to give birth, on the ashes of the
> old, the new world that we want, that we need, that we deserve.
> (EZLN, 2013e)

Regarding the political principle of commanding by obeying, Lenkersdorf
identifies its political meaning derived from the linguistic matrix:

> *mandar'ay.* The word *mandar* is derived ... from the Spanish verb
> *mandar* (to command). In Tojolabal it has the exclusive meaning
> of *giving orders.* In combination with the stative verb *'ay,* however,
> it corresponds to *receiving orders.* A translation of the partial
> phrase would be: *We give orders to our authorities.* (2005, p. 80)

Contrary to the principle of liberal democracy in which the right of political representation of the majority is delegated to a single individual backed
by a party, in Zapatismo, the epistemic principle of commanding by obeying
legitimizes the collective voice, in the social and political direction of the
movement, by listening to the people (Barbosa, 2015). Thus, the assemblies
constitute the collective subject *par excellence* and the space for building
consensus among all, which generates a cathartic effect on decision-making
and the political conduct of decisions. However, this process of dialogue
is only possible because of the existence of the "we" as an epistemic matrix
of socio-political organization and of an intersubjectivity that conforms
to certain principles of community sociability. The strengthening of the

assemblies as the collective voice of the Zapatista base communities allows the consolidation of the democratic principle of *mandar obedeciendo* (commanding while obeying), that is, to ensure that all the authorities elected by the communities, in the civil and military spheres, execute the agreements that come out of the assemblies in the social and political spheres. This allows us to understand the relationship between *power* and *us,* since, within the framework of commanding by obeying, the principle of horizontality prevails in intersubjective relations in social and political fields, that is, the distribution of power among the totality of the people (Lenkersdorf, 2005).

In Zapatista political praxis, popular and class autonomy is anti-capitalist in principle:

> We believe, and it is clear, that to be anti-capitalist it is to seize the means of production, the land and factories, and pass them into the hands of the working people, so that they are the property of the working people, and thus to put an end to the exploiters, the bosses, the capitalists. With struggle and the praxis, in farm work, of the *compañeros* and *compañeras* of the Zapatista peoples, it is clear how anti-capitalism should be. Seize, remove, recover the means of production and organize ourselves for decision making and govern ourselves, and if we don't do this, neoliberalism will reign in Mexico and in the world. We think and believe that uniting the workers of the countryside and the city, and organizing ourselves under the idea that the people are in charge and take all the means of production into their hands, is the way out of this savage capitalism that reigns today. This is one of the characteristics of our organization of the EZLN and one of the most important things about the Sixth Declaration of the Lacandon Jungle, which is the guide for our passage in the Other Campaign and in the Zezta International: anti-capitalism. (EZLN, 2007a)

In their first public documents, the EZLN demanded that "regions, indigenous communities and municipalities govern themselves with political, economic and cultural autonomy" (1994, p. 180); that is, they demanded a territorial dimension of autonomy. Likewise, they also demanded, in the political sphere, "a new federal pact that puts an end to centralism and allows the autonomy of indigenous communities and municipalities" (EZLN, 1994, p. 261).

In different documents and books produced by the Zapatistas, we find their method and theory erected in a permanent dialogue of knowledge with the epistemic and ontological matrices of the Mayan languages and with the legacy of critical social theory, but also from a creative capacity that, in the words of Subcomandante Insurgente Moisés, impelled them to invent, while imagining and creating (EZLN, 2015a). A philosophical and pedagogical principle of this process is the pedagogy of the question, as explained by Moisés:

> Questions are important. As is our Zapatista way, they are more important than the answers .... It's about making you realize that what interests the Zapatistas is not certainties, but doubts. Because we think that certainties immobilize, that is, leading one to remain tranquil and contented, as if one has already arrived or already knows what we are looking for. On the other hand, doubts, questions make one move, search and feel dissatisfied, as if day and nights do not pass by. And the struggles *from below and on the left* are born of disagreements, doubts and unrest. If one is satisfied, it's because we're waiting to be told what to do or have already been told what to do. If one is dissatisfied, one is looking for what to do.[7] (EZLN, 2015b)

On the other hand, to understand the contradictions of capital on the threshold of the twenty-first century:

> One would have to revisit Marx, Lenin, Gramsci, Mao, Trotsky, Che Guevara and other revolutionaries, because no responsible proposal for radical change in our time can ignore the analysis and teachings of these revolutionaries and the movements they led. (EZLN, 1996, p. 51)

Now, when the Zapatistas talk about autonomy, about the construction of this *very different*, unique Zapatista autonomy, they affirm that "there is no book where we are guided on how to achieve autonomy in our government, there is no book that directs us, we learn through doing" (EZLN, 2013c, p.7). It is through the Zapatista journey, asking questions, that the communities, together with the EZLN, are paving the way in a dialectical relationship between new theory and new praxis. It is the dimension of praxis in a communitarian sense. They say there is no intellectual vanguard. The revolution is "like a construction of humanity" (EZLN, 2013c, p. 25).

In this regard, Jacinto, education promoter, MAREZ El Work, Caracol V, says:

What is going to be the ideological politics in our resistance? We think that change is not achieved from the government, but that change is achieved from the grassroots, from the people, when the people are the ones who decide, the ones who give their opinion. (EZLN, 2013d, p. 73)

Zapatismo offers us both political theory and the most creative and innovative contemporary territorializing praxis. It is a praxis that is coherent with discourse and ideology. Hence, we argue that Zapatismo constitutes the movement that is most coherent between discourse and practice in the world today.

Zapatismo and the Sounds of Silence

In other expressions of its political discourse, in its dialogue with society, the EZLN makes eloquent use of *silence* as a communication device, very much in the style of great authors and Nobel Laureates in literature (Kouachi, 2018; de la Peña Martínez, 2003), although from a different ontology. In the case of the Zapatistas, silence is an inheritance of Mayan philosophy, where the body also communicates: "What they tell us without speaking and without teaching" (Rajchenberg and Héau-Lambert, 2004). In the Fifth Declaration of the Lacandon Jungle, the Zapatistas begin by quoting the sacred Popol Vuh: "We are the darkness that shines, the silence that speaks, the mask that shows, the resistance that lives" (EZLN, 1998b).

On numerous occasions the EZLN have responded with silence to statements (and/or actions) addressed to them by the state, politicians, the media, famous intellectuals and so on. Enrique Rajchenberg and Catheryne Héau-Lambert explain:

Just as the biblical word comes from God, in the secular world the state claims that function. Hence, "the state never stops talking." The state is not only a monopoly of force; it is also a monopoly in the space of the word. It is not that it forbids speaking, but that it tries to make everyone speak as it does: it dictates the codes of language .... The state speaks incessantly because it assumes that others listen, and listening in Latin is called *obaudire*, which in English translates as "obey." (2004, p. 3)

The Zapatista silence communicates many things, but the most obvious is that *certain things do not deserve a response*. In these cases, which are common among states and the intelligentsia obedient to them, there is no better response than no response. In the Zapatista insurrection, not only is the word that was silenced recovered, but also the uses and meanings of silence are recovered. In this sense, Zapatista silence, used at opportune moments, is almost the opposite of silencing. It is a deliberate and eloquent use of the word (Rajchenberg and Héau-Lambert, 2004). The Fifth Declaration continues:

> The Zapatistas turned silence into a weapon of struggle that they were not familiar with and against which they could do nothing, and against our silence the stinging lies, the bullets, the bombs, the blows crashed again and again. Just as after the fighting of January 1994 we discovered in the word a weapon, now we did so with silence. While the government offered everyone threats, death and destruction, we were able to learn and teach ourselves, and teach ourselves another way of fighting, that with reason, truth and history, you can fight and win. (EZLN, 1998b)

For example, on December 21, 2012, more than 40,000 Zapatista people from the five Zapatista *caracoles* that existed at that time held silent marches in the Chiapas cities of Ocosingo, San Cristóbal de Las Casas, Palenque, Altamirano and Las Margaritas:

> The event burst into daily life, and symbolism reappeared powerfully, as they chose the last day of the cycle, the 13th Baktun; for many it was to be the end of the world, while for others the beginning of a new era, the shedding of skin, renewal. In all the central plazas the Zapatistas erected small stages upon which Tzeltales, Tzotziles, Choles, Tojolabales, Zoques, Mames and mestizos, with their traditional bandanas and balaclavas, climbed with their fists raised, demonstrating discipline and organization, in rows and in silence. It was a political action that said, "We are here."
>
> (Sánchez Ramírez, 2018, p. 591)

At the end of the March of Silence, the CCRI-CG issued the following communiqué:

> Have you heard?
>
> It's the sound of your world collapsing.
>
> It's ours reappearing.
>
> The day that was day was night.
>
> And night will be the day that will be the day.

DEMOCRACY!

FREEDOM!

JUSTICE!

From the mountains of the Mexican Southeast.

Clandestine Indigenous Revolutionary Committee — General Command of the EZLN,

Subcomandante Insurgente Marcos,

Mexico, December 2012. (EZLN, 2012)

This March of Silence was emblematic of the Zapatista pedagogy aimed at society as a whole: it teaches us to *listen in a different way*. Among those who follow the EZLN closely, the interpretation of silences — and words — is a much-needed art and political tool. At the same time, as highlighted above, the Zapatistas emphasize the centrality of critical thinking, which draws on the different sources of historical struggles:

> We think that we must have good thinking to get organized. In other words, you need theory, critical thinking. With critical thinking we analyze the ways of the enemy, of those who oppress us .... With critical thinking we see what our path is like, what our steps are like. That is why we are calling the whole of the Sixth to hold meetings of thought, of analysis, of theory, of how they see their world, their struggle, their history. We call on you to make your own seedbeds and share with us what you plant there. (EZLN, 2015a, pp. 348–349)

Finally, we highlight the essay by Subcomandante Insurgente Galeano (2017) entitled *Kamegusha: April Is Also Tomorrow*, in which the Cuban Revolution is recognized as a central reference in the international struggle for socialism and the emancipation of the peoples. Recognizing Cuba means recognizing the legacy of other revolutionary processes, including the alma mater of the Soviet Revolution of 1917.

Zapatista Political Ontology and the Defence of Territory

In 2023, the Zapatista Movement celebrated the thirtieth anniversary of the armed insurgency and the consolidation of autonomy as a political project. A fundamental step in the political trajectory of Zapatismo was the gradual recovery of land and the building of territorial autonomy in the

MAREZ. As mentioned, the date of the armed insurgency, January 1, 1994, was deliberately chosen to coincide with the entry into force of NAFTA, which inaugurated a new stage of neo-extractivist territorial expropriation. With NAFTA and other "free trade" agreements there was a reconfiguration in the geopolitics of capitalism, not only in the context of the Americas but on a global scale. Land continued to play its historical role in the context of the agrarian question. However, territory came to have a strategic value in capitalism by dispossession, and thus, the articulation of free trade agreements became the imperialist modality adopted for the expanded reproduction of capital in the Global South. In the case of NAFTA, Mexico was a strategic country for three reasons: 1. it has abundant resources, like water, oil, minerals, wind and solar energy, and biodiversity and, therefore, is a valuable source of raw materials; 2. it has a natural transcontinental connection via Central America, which could facilitate the flow of trade; and 3. by participating in a trilateral treaty, conditions were created for the imposition of a regulatory framework for territories of interest to capital that the Mexican government would have to comply with, for example, by granting concessions to Canadian and US mining companies.

The modification of Article 27 of the Constitution, which shook the very foundations of rural Mexico, was one of the changes in land regulation made to pave the way for NAFTA. As previously noted, there was ongoing concern in the communities with this change in Mexican agrarian law. During the International Seminar on Critical Thinking in the Face of the Capitalist Hydra, Subcomandante Insurgente Moisés affirmed: "The capitalist system set a trap when they modified Article 27 so that the ejidos can be privatized, because what they want is to be able to buy, sell or rent the Mother Earth" (EZLN, 2015a, p. 79). In a similar vein, when analyzing issues of land and territory, the following statement was made in 2014 by a member of the JBG of Caracole II, during the First World Festival of Resistance and Rebellion against Capitalism:[8]

> They make laws that only benefit the transnationals. With this law they created they can easily enter our communal lands, without the permission of us as indigenous peoples, even if we are the legitimate owners. Based on this law they say that they now have the right to enter our lands. (Author field notes)

Zapatista autonomy includes the defence of land, territory and Mother Earth; after three decades of the daily building of autonomy, the power held by Zapatista political and symbolic territoriality is clear. It conforms to an ontological and epistemic framework that is imbedded in subjectivity, that is, in the intersubjective relationships woven between themselves and with nature, giving different meanings to territory, as well as to existence and coexistence in it. As with other aspects of Zapatista thought discussed in this book, the expression of this territoriality can be found in categories that emerge from Mayan languages and philosophical thought (Barbosa, 2015). In the ontology of Mesoamerican indigenous peoples, cosmovision expresses a social and philosophical logic that brings together their conceptions of time, history, ecology, intersubjective relations and relations with nature and can even be considered a phenomenological model that offers a particular vision of the natural, supernatural and human or social worlds (Broda, 2003).

Language plays a bridging role, providing a gateway into the world and culture of indigenous peoples by grasping the various meanings and symbolisms that express the way they belong the world and how they interpret it (Lenkersdorf, 2004). The sense of intersubjectivity in the indigenous cultural and linguistic structure permeates all spheres and spaces in which their worldview manifests itself — socio-cultural, spiritual, economic and political — demonstrating the inseparable link between language and lived reality. Language reveals how indigenous peoples weave conceptions, interpretive visions and meanings about the world and themselves in their interaction with it. In this way of seeing the world lies the process of shaping a political intersubjectivity and a social and collective identity as peoples (Barbosa, 2015).

As we have highlighted throughout this book, an outstanding legacy of Zapatismo is its social theory permeated by a variety of concepts that are central to Zapatista ontology and epistemology and which are the foundations of its political theory and praxis (Barbosa, 2016). We have identified some of them from the Mayan languages spoken in the Zapatista territories, which express an ontology that is antagonistic to the ontology of capital (Barbosa, 2024). We now present how Zapatismo conceives the defence of territory, and in particular of communal territory, based on a political ontology that sets in motion key concepts of the Zapatista ontological and epistemic matrix. To do this, we use the method of *o'tán-puy* or *o'tán-tot* (heart-*caracol*) as a dialectical approach to situate the concepts that emerge from Zapatista ontology, that guide its political territoriality in confronting the ontology of capital and that therefore make it an anti-capitalist and anti-imperialist struggle (Barbosa, 2024).

A basic concept used in the Mayan Tojolabal language is Sak'an — Earth — also used to mean something that lives or even a prolonged life (Guerrero Martínez, 2022). From the Tojolabal perspective, Mother

Earth is a living being, fulfilling the primordial task of generating life and producing food. We also find the Tojolabal concept of *altzil*, understood as a principle of life, that is, "it gives life to people, animals, plants and all things by dwelling in them, because there is nothing that does not have a heart/that does not have life (Lenkersdorf, 2004, p. 54). Another spelling of *altzil* is *ja 'altsili* — everything lives. In this conceptual pair, we identify an epistemic break with the Western approach to nature, with its separation between "living" and "dead" nature. In other words, in the Mayan worldview, everything has life, everything lives. Thus, the dimension of life includes human beings but also fauna, flora, waters, mountains, rocks, caves, stars and so on (Lenkersdorf, 2008). From an epistemic point of view, to consider that everything lives is to recognize that there is no separation between life and death.

The perspective of a living Earth, Mother Earth as a living being, expresses an ontological counterpoint to capital's ontological understanding of territory as a source of commodities. When analyzing the threats posed by the advance of capital over their territories, a member of the JBG of Caracole V said: "They want to do away with taking care of our Mother Earth, and with the way we relate to her as indigenous peoples."[9] A JBG member from Caracol I added:

> These neoliberal savages are coming with everything to destroy and plunder all our natural wealth and take it wherever they want, to get richer. They are coming with everything to dispossess us and evict us where we, for thousands of years, have been, are and will continue to be guardians of Mother Earth. (Author field notes)

Two concepts from the Tseltal language reveal the ontology of Mayan sociability: *o'tan* (heart); *stael* and *ch'ulel* (soul-spirit-consciousness) (López Intzín, 2013) or *o'tanil* (heart) (Pérez Moreno, 2019). According to Juan López Intzín (2013), these concepts express the basis of the Mayan cosmovision and community sociability in their relationship with each other, with the community, with the cosmos and with nature. The *o'tan*, as the core of the Maya-Tzeltal worldview, shapes the understanding of life and individual and collective positioning in the world, based on an epistemic foundation of existence that gives meanings to the ways of feeling-thinking and feeling-knowing in and with the world. For María Patricia Pérez Moreno (2019), the *o'tanil* alludes not only to the heart as a physiological organ, but to a *stael*, that is, a different way of relating to everything around us, be it people, animals, plants, forces of nature or the cosmos. It is the place where ideas, thoughts, feelings and actions are born — therefore, a philosophizing of existence of everything that exists and inhabits the earth. Thus, the *o'tanil* expresses dimensions of the "life-existence of people, animals, plants, goddesses and gods; as well as organizational aspects of the community, moral and ethical values, wisdom, identity, honesty and spirituality .... Everything is alive and has a heart" (Pérez Moreno, 2021, p. 40).

From an ontological point of view, *ch'ulel* is fundamental to life and is also a constituent part of the waters and mountains (Pitarch Ramón, 1996). As Pérez Moreno (2021, p. 45) explains, "Water is the moisture of the head and heart of the mountains and caves; water is what keeps us alive .... We are grateful for the greenness and freshness of the water that makes possible the growth of people's food." The *o'tan, o'tanil* (heart) has an ontological root in Mayan thinking-feeling, which is fundamental to their philosophical and political thought, their socio-cultural formation and an aesthetic of resistance that is expressed in the defence of territories and the commons (Barbosa, 2019b). On the other hand, *stael* and *ch'ulel* are not uniquely human attributes. From the Mayan perspective, everything that exists in nature, or even that has been created by human beings has *stael* and *ch'ulel*, that is, a spirit that exists: a house has *ch'ulel*, as does an animal, a mountain, a weaving loom and so on.

These categories of Mayan linguistics express an existential unity that breaks with the modern Western conception of an anthropocentric world, that is, one with human beings at the centre of the universe. For the indigenous Mayan peoples, this ontological foundation guides the meanings attributed to their own existence and the world itself, a reflexive action in the construction of consciousness that is not limited solely to reason, in the Western sense, that is, an understanding of human existence based on separate logics, dissociated into a rational and an emotional dimension. On the contrary, from the Mayan perspective, the heart is the ontological and epistemic core of their worldview, which, in turn, links a unified dimension of reason, consciousness, feeling and emotions. As Subcomandante Insurgente Marcos pointed out:

> When we Zapatistas speak, we put the red heart that we collectively beat in front of us. To understand what we say, do and will do is impossible if our word is not felt. It is very difficult to feel with the head and think with the heart. (EZLN, 2007b, p. 322)

According to the Popol Wuj, the sacred book of the K'iché peoples of Guatemala, the heart is the place of enunciation for the creation of life, thought and words; the place from which feeling and reason emanate. For the Mayan peoples of the Mesoamerican region, the Popol Wuj, as a sacred writing, is a basic reference of their cosmovision and *cosmovivencia* (experience of living together in harmony with the other living and non-living beings with whom we humans share the cosmos); it contains the foundations of ancestral rationality, human creation by the will of the creator gods and animals, their connection with the four elements, their conception of time, life and death, as well as an interpretation of human beings as a fraction of the totality of life existing in nature. In different territorial defence processes articulated by Mesoamerican indigenous movements, we find direct references to the Popol Wuj (Barbosa, 2019). Likewise, the Popol Wuj is present in the aesthetics of the Zapatista resistance, such as in documents and symbologies in their territories. In the training process of autonomous Zapatista schools, references to Popol Wuj are in their learning materials, such as the Arte en Rebeldía (Art in Rebellion) textbook (EZLN, 2006).

Based on these concepts, the attribute of reason, of one's own philosophy, does not exclude the emotions, feelings and spiritualities that are also constituent elements of human beings and their coexistence with each other and with other beings within the material and immaterial planes of life. Before becoming an abstract operation of reason, thoughts and knowledge first pass through the heart; in the Zapatista perspective, the thoughts and knowledge are heartfelt (Barbosa, 2014). Thus, it is common to hear in Zapatista discourse that they express their word as being born from the heart.

Another central concept is *'ab'i* (listening). For Lenkersdorf (2008), *'ab'i* represents listening that incorporates ways of feeling and thinking from the perspective of the other, in other words, in a reciprocal relationship of "we" — *tik*. Listening to the other presupposes the ability to put oneself in their place, while at the same time listening to understand the arguments that structure the position of the person being listened to. Therefore, the process of listening requires an ability to understand the words and feelings expressed by others. *'Ab'i* is a central concept for understanding, for example, the seven Zapatista principles.

This entire conceptual body expresses a crucial Zapatista ontology in the understanding of territory as a constitutive locus of life and is essential in the process of territorial defence of Mother Earth and of the commons. This ontology is built on the method articulated by the dialectical pair heart-*caracol* or *o'tán-puy* or *o'tán-tot*, the core of the multiple meanings attributed to the ancestral experience of the community social fabric in its coexistence with the territory. Although the EZLN's armed insurgency was the crucial act of defending the territory in anticipation of capital's imminent offensive with NAFTA, it is the method of *o'tán-puy* or *o'tán-tot*, the dialectical movement of an experiential ontology of the heart-*caracol*, that demarcates and ensures the daily experience of autonomy in their territories, in the ancestral confrontation of the "ontocide" imposed by colonialism and capitalism. By ontocide, we mean the killing off of the collective memories of peoples, memories of who they are, where they came from and how they differ from hegemonic, dominant cultures. The fact that the Zapatista peoples are, first and foremost, Mayan peoples, activates, within their political struggle, a common collective *ch'ulel* (Barbosa, 2024) in defence of territorial autonomy.

There is an aspect of Zapatista social and political theory rooted in the *o'tán-puy* or *o'tán-tot* method (Barbosa, 2024), a dialectical approach that allows us to understand other dimensions of the Zapatista ontology articulated by: 1. an onto-epistemic basis that springs from the cosmovision and conceptual matrices of the mother tongues present in the Zapatista territories, to ground their philosophical and theoretical-political thought; and 2. a political praxis that orients Zapatista territoriality. In the field of Zapatista ontology, the method of *o'tán-puy* or *o'tán-tot* allows us to identify concepts that reveal ontological dimensions of territory and Mother Earth which sustain Zapatista political subjectivity in the material and spiritual planes and which are appropriated in the political praxis of Zapatismo in the defence of territory and the commons. Likewise, the method of *o'tán-puy* or *o'tán-tot* provides us with some analytical keys to the Zapatista ontology that establishes a political territoriality of confrontation to the ontology of capital, which makes it an anti-capitalist and anti-imperialist struggle. The political proposal of "communal territory," announced by the EZLN during the commemorations of the thirtieth anniversary of the Zapatista uprising at the end of 2023, placed at the centre of their political analysis a dialectical articulation of the onto-epistemic foundations of a praxis that challenges the attempts at what we call the ontocide of capital (Barbosa, 2022), at the same time that it is anti-capitalist and anti-imperialist.

One of the premises of capitalism is to consolidate a rationality based on private property, the alienation of labour power, the appropriation of surplus value and commodity fetishism. However, the success of the development of capitalism does not lie solely in the material processes of expropriation and exploitation inherent in the social relations of production. Capitalism needs to consolidate itself from a subjective point of view as well, with the individualization of social relations, a process instituted in two ways: 1. in the imposition of modern Western capitalist rationality based on anthropocentrism; and 2. in the creation of the modern state. The first was historically based on ontocide, or cultural erasure, a method used to delegitimize, inferiorize and deny other rationalities based on dialectical articulations between reason-feelings-emotions, as well as human existence in coexistence with nature (Barbosa, 2022). In the case of the creation of the modern state, it constituted the ideal form of coercion and domination for capitalism, of a hierarchical and class nature, established on a national and international level as a mechanism of regulation and control. This is how the ontology of capital and its strategic interest in the territories of the Global South are advancing at a dizzying pace.

Aware of the subjectivation undertaken by capitalism, the Zapatistas warn: "Now they have realized that in the hills, the mountains, there is another commodity for them … it is the wealth of nature. So they start organizing themselves to evict us again …. That is, to plunder us, to evict us, because they want this wealth" (EZLN, 2015a, p. 79). The Zapatista ontology breaks with the ontology intrinsic to the modern capitalist Western paradigm, starting with the negation of the modern state and the understanding of nature as a commodity and/or a producer of commodities.

In the war of plunder we find a clash between antagonistic ontological paradigms. In the Zapatista ontology, the rivers, the mountains, the wind and the earth, to name but a few of the beings that exist in the territory, are living beings, they have an *altzil*, a life principle. For capital, they are likely to become commodities. For a mining company, for example, it doesn't matter if there is a *ch'ulel* or a *stael* in the mountains that it wants to destroy in order to extract ore, preferably with a long river next to it so that it has water at its disposal, which it will poison with mine tailings. However, the Zapatista ontology expresses an existential subjectivation that challenges the ontocidal character of capital and gives meaning to territorial defence, the commons and the good life — *lekil kuxlejal* (full, dignified and just). In the daily experience of autonomy, decisions about the territory are not delegated to governments or capital. On the contrary, autonomous governments understand that the whole community contributes to caring for the territory — *kanantayel lum k'inal* because it contains the totality of life existence (Mora, 2023).

The ontological sense of an *altzil* as the principle of life on Sak'an (Earth) — a principle of vital existence — underpins the defence of its territories, as we can see during the twenty-fifth anniversary of the armed uprising in 2019, in the message of Subcommandante Insurgente Moisés:

We are going to confront; we are not going to allow this project of destruction to happen here .... We are going to defend what we have built and we are demonstrating to the people of Mexico and the world that we are the ones who are here, women and men; we are not going to allow them to come and destroy us, are we? ... We know what Mother Earth is, we have been living with her [under colonialism] for five hundred and twenty years. We know, we know, not those who do not know and have not felt the sweat, who think they know .... We are not afraid of capitalism, of the landowner, of the new landowner; are we afraid of him? (EZLN, 2019)

On the same celebratory evening, the CCRI also issued its statement:

We will not allow any project that destroys the life of humanity and causes the death of our Mother Earth, because behind all this are the interests of the great national and transnational capitalists .... From 1492 to this 2018, 525 years have passed of resistance and rebellion against the great foreign and Mexican humiliations; they have never been able to exterminate us. We, those of brown blood, skin the colour of Mother Earth, reiterate that we are here, and we will continue to be here. (EZLN, 2019)

During the launching of the Global Campaign for the Defence of Autonomous Indigenous and Peasant Lands and Territories, in 2007, Zapatista Comandante Keli presented the concept of territory: "For indigenous, peasant and rural peoples, land and territory are more than just sources of work and food; they are also culture, community, history, ancestors, dreams, future, life and mother" (EZLN, 2007c). We also find the ontological meaning attributed to territory in the perspective of Zapatista Comandante Tacho:

We, indigenous peoples and peasants, historically have our roots in these territories, we relate to them, through Mother Earth. Here we produce our food to live, here we are born, here we develop, here we multiply and coexist, with the mountains, with the rivers, with the air, with the life of nature itself, the seas, the springs, as well as all living beings with the right to life, as well as the resources of the subsoil. We, the indigenous peoples, peasants, take care of and love our Mother Earth and we have demonstrated it for centuries. Never in the history of humanity have we, the indigenous peoples, peasants, done any serious damage to Mother Earth, never. (EZLN, 2007b)

From Land to Non-property Communal Territory

For Zapatismo, a central element in confronting capital is the recovery of land, which they have done through the declaration of radical autonomy and the Revolutionary Agrarian Laws. Communal and collective owner-ship of the land is essential for defending their territories since it enables communities to avoid the condition of subalternization, which they were subject to when their means of production were expropriated from them. When organized peoples have control of their territory, they are more likely to prevent capital from violently assaulting it.

In the last decade, the Zapatista Movement has emphasized that the repro-duction of capital occurs via the historical mechanisms of war and plunder:

> Capital has begun to replace neoliberalism as a theoretical-ideological justification with the war of annihilation of large populations to achieve the "welfare" of modern society. War is not a breakdown of the machine, it is the "regular maintenance" that will ensure its functioning and duration. The radical reduction of demand compensates for the limitations of supply .... The con-quest of territories brought the exponential growth of "surplus," "excluded" or "expendable" people. The wars for the division of the spoils of territory continue. Wars have a double advantage: they revive war production and its lucrative subsidiaries, and they eliminate these surplus populations in an expeditious and irremediable way. (EZLN, 2023b)

The logic that sustains capitalism in the twenty-first century causes crises to deepen, which the Zapatistas refer to as a storm: "Capitalism, says Zapatismo, is war. And in its current stage, capitalism is a war against humanity as a whole, against the planet as a whole ... weeping blood and mud through every pore, from head to toe" (EZLN, 2015a, p. 316). In the Seminar on Critical Thinking in the Face of the Capitalist Hydra referenced earlier, the Zapatistas carried out an analysis of the genealogy of capitalism and delved into the dimensions of spoliation in order to elucidate, in the light of political economy, its stages and impacts on indigenous and peasant territories. They affirmed "that a catastrophe is coming in every sense of the word, a storm" (EZLN, 2015a, p. 27). From the Zapatista perspective, the storm manifests itself as a deep crisis, especially the climate crisis:

> An economic crisis like never before. What we see now are only the first rains, the worst is yet to come. The economists at the top have gone from pointing out that the turbulence will be over

in months, to anticipating that it will take years. They are not allowed to tell the truth: they have no idea where this crisis will lead. Because it turns out that it is not only an economic crisis. It has to be multiplied by unnatural environmental catastrophes, since they are the effect of an unnatural cause: the transformation of everything, even the elementary basics — water, air, light and shadow, earth and sky — into commodities. (EZLN, 2015a)

In this century, we are seeing the advance of a political-ideological discourse that defends the promotion of so-called renewable technologies as an alternative to the climate crisis. However, as the Zapatista Movement emphasizes, this is a false alternative. They argue that there is no crisis of capitalism, but crises caused by capitalism, which always seeks its own mechanisms of reproduction within the contradictions it has created. In a scenario of environmental collapse,

the catastrophe is not followed by the end of the capitalist system, but by a different form of its predatory character. The future of capital is the same as its patriarchal past and present: exploitation, repression, dispossession and contempt. For every crisis, the system always has a war at hand to solve that crisis. Therefore: it is not possible to delineate or build an alternative to the collapse beyond our own survival as native communities. (EZLN, 2023b)

The critical analysis of the genealogy of capitalism present in Zapatista political praxis reveals the historical continuum of the expanded reproduction of capital, anchored in the incessant search for a territorial monopoly and the implementation of the ontology of capital through ontocide. With Zapatista autonomy, their territories are free of the mega-enterprises driven by NAFTA (and its successor USMCA). However, other threats are lurking, such as violence from paramilitary forces and organized crime (the armed branch of capital), which makes Mexico one of the countries with the highest levels of violence, especially in the countryside, and which manifests in a significant number of missing persons, murdered leaders and journalists, and extremely violent murders, with dismemberments, beheadings and public displays of corpses. The escalation of violence in Mexico coincided with the signing of NAFTA and is more forcefully located in territories of interest to capital, which makes violence, according to Zapatismo, a weapon of plunder (EZLN, 2015a).

Aware of this political context and in solidarity with other struggles that directly confront these multiple forms of violence, in 2023 Zapatismo began openly calling for the construction of "communal territory" in areas they call "the common," or "non-property," a totally indigenous political proposal with Mayan roots. In one of their communiqués, the Zapatistas reflect on the ambiguities and hidden (or not so hidden) traps present in the distribution of land by the state as a mechanism for controlling territories and for provoking internal conflicts within communities and thus weakening any possibility of collective resistance:

> The problems, the internal divisions, the arguments and the fights all came when the property titles arrived. It is not that before there were no problems; it is that they were solved by coming to informal local agreements. That is to say, if there is a paper that says it is the property of one person, then the land has to be divided into pieces for the different applicants. It has to be parceled out so that there can be several versions of the same piece of paper. There is no real redistribution of land, the same property is just divided into pieces. (EZLN, 2023d; see Part 3 of the Postsript in this volume)

One of the historical functions of the modern state is to regulate private property for the full development of capitalism. Private property is a way of parceling out the land and parceling out the territory. It is also a dismemberment of the social fabric and of the feeling of belonging to the land and the territory. By calling for the construction of "communal territory," the Zapatista Movement is inviting us not to own the land. This may seem contradictory when we see above that land ownership is an important element in territorial defence. However, the Zapatista Movement analyzes that the state has understood how to instrumentalize the law as a mechanism of control, especially during elections, when a discourse is created that coerces votes in exchange for rights, including the right to land. This has been observed in different Latin American countries, when electoral campaigns use the vote as a bargaining chip, with promises of land reform and the demarcation of indigenous and afro-descendent territories, among other promises that are rarely fulfilled. Meanwhile, the Zapatistas warn that property law is a mechanism for territorial dispossession:

> The law constitutes "legal" theft. With laws, an army of lawyers, authorities corrupted with a few banknotes and a legal system made by those at the top to leave out those at the bottom, thousands of hectares are shamelessly stolen. These go from being dedicated to cultivation to modifying their use for tourism and for exploitation of mining, timber and water. (EZLN, 2015a, p. 289)

It is for this reason that the Zapatistas launched their 2023 proposal of "non-property," in which they propose to establish

> extensions of reclaimed land as communal territory. That is, without being property. Neither private, nor ejido, nor communal, nor federal, nor state, nor corporate, nor anything else. A non-ownership of the land. One could say "land without papers." Then, in those lands that are going to be seized, if they ask who owns that land or who is the owner, the answer will be "nobody's," or "nobody," that is to say, "the common people's." … There will be no commissariat or ejidal agent to buy, kill, disappear. What there will be are people who work and take care of those lands. And who defend them. (EZLN, 2023d)

To materialize this "communal territory," the Zapatista Movement proposes the dialogical method to reach a common agreement between communities (EZLN, 2023d): "An important part is that, in order to achieve this, there has to be an agreement between the inhabitants regardless of whether they are political party supporters or Zapatistas." They elaborated:

> And what we did was, then, to propose a path to be able to weather the storm and get to the other side safely. And to not walk that path alone as Zapatistas, but together as the original peoples that we are …. Let's say that we see it as necessary in order to be able to face the storm. (EZLN, 2023d)

This 2023 proposal was preceded by the announcement of the following new structure and political configuration of Zapatista territory in general: 1. The JBGs and MAREZ would be replaced by local autonomous governments (GALs) — the main location for administering autonomy, coordinated by autonomous local agents and commissariats chosen by the local assembly. Each GAL was to be responsible for the functioning of autonomous structures and institutions (schools, clinics, etc.), as well as for the relationship established with non-Zapatista communities and other organizations; 2. collectives of autonomous Zapatista governments (CGAZs) were to be created on an as need basis, with the power of convening, when necessary, the assembly of authorities of each community within a region for decision making and deliberations; and 3. assemblies of collectives of autonomous Zapatista governments (ACGAZs) would operate over a broader area (see the Postscript in this volume).

This new structure of autonomy is the fruit of a decade of reflection and internal debates on the successes, weaknesses and challenges in building and consolidating Zapatista autonomy. This reorganization has a greater horizontality in the structure and coordination of autonomy in the territories. The somewhat top-down or pyramid structure of governance based on the MAREZ and the JBGs is being transformed into more community-level governance, represented by the GALs (see EZLN, 2023d, and the Postscript in this volume).

Although the reorganization and the declaration of communal territory came as a surprise to many who follow the Zapatista struggle, we believe that there are at least four levels of analysis for understanding that struggle (Barbosa, 2024): First, as we have seen, before they were Zapatista territories, the territories were made up of Mayan peoples, who, in the historical process of their resistance, incorporated several strategies of struggle, including armed struggle. The onto-epistemic paradigm that governs their territories maintains and/or recovers ancestral forms of self-government and the organization of socio-cultural life on a non-capitalist communal basis. The very existence of autonomous governments is a distinct form and predates that guided by the modern Western state. Private land ownership is a colonial and capitalist invention. Therefore, it is possible to consolidate consensus and agreements between Zapatistas and non-Zapatistas, since territorial life in shared and/or border areas is governed by forms of indigenous self-government, which predate the foundation of the Zapatista Movement.

The second level of analysis concerns the advance of organized crime in the territories, which requires the construction of community strategies to confront it. The EZLN is a military form of territorial defence. There are currently other forms of territorial defence in Mexico organized by indigenous communities, such as community police and so-called "self-defences." In the face of violent threats from organized crime, it is essential to establish alliances to defend territories. The reconfiguration of the Zapatista territory with GALs and CGAZs allows for the strengthening of grassroots unity in the territories and a closer dialogue with non-Zapatista communities, which can be strategic in territorial defence.

The third analytical plane to highlight is the anti-capitalist nature of "communal territory," as it suggests a radical break with the basis for capitalism's existence, defined by the creation of private property and the private ownership of land. With the advance of capitalism through dispossession, territory becomes the object of capital's interest, and the more land is divided up, the greater the fragmentation of the social fabric, caused either by organized crime using violence to expel communities from their territories, or by state regulation, which grants land titles so that communities can sell their piece of land to companies at derisory prices, out of fear or even because they can no longer afford to live there. Thus, the strategy of "communal territory" can be a way of strengthening the social cohesion of different organizations and movements that cohabit a territory in resistance to these contemporary forms of expropriation and in the defence of this territory.

The fourth and final level of analysis consists of making "communal territory" the vehicle for confronting capital's war on life, which represents a veritable crusade against nature in order to further mineral, oil, water and wind and solar energy extraction. The Mayan ontological dimensions articulated by Zapatista political territoriality converge with the territorial defence processes of other organizations and movements that are on their borders or even share their territories. In a communal territory, it is not only possible to link a common daily enjoyment of the territory but also to activate a common collective *ch'ulel* in territorial defence and in defence of life, not only human life but also nature itself. To this end, there is a political subjectivation of the territory delimited by Zapatista political ontology, in which the method of *o'tán-puy* or *o'tán-tot* is in itself the dialectical movement of an experiential ontology of the heart-*caracol* in defence of the territory and of Mother Earth. In this sense, communal territory can also be interpreted as a call to a political subjectivity for the weaving of life, that is, a community of existence (Barbosa, 2024).

In the ontology of capital, the temporality of commodity exploitation confers a durability to the use of territory that is similar to the planned obsolescence of many products. Thus, different territories in the Global South have been affected by the impacts of ecocidal policy, becoming sacrifice zones for capital, and when they no longer serve a purpose for big capital, they become disposable, abandoned. In the capitalist ontology, a balanced coexistence between human beings and nature is not possible:

> Capital has turned our relationship with nature into a confrontation, a war of plunder and destruction. The objective of this war is the annihilation of the opposite, nature in this case (humanity included). With the criterion of "programmed obsolescence" (or "planned obsolescence"), the commodity "human beings" expires in every war. The logic of capital is that of the highest profit at maximum speed. This turns the system into a gigantic waste machine, including human beings … [while] indigenous communities are the "strange enemy" that dares to "desecrate" the soil of the system's ranch. (EZLN, 2023b)

The consequences of the ontology of capital are already being experienced in the tragedies resulting from the climate crisis. The Zapatista

Movement asserts that this ontology of capital impacts the balance of nature, negatively transforming the conditions needed for existence:

> You have already explained it here. You have told us what you see in your Tzeltal, Tzotzil, Cho'ol, Tojolabal, Mame, Zoque, and Quiché areas. You already know what is happening to Mother Earth because you live and work on her. You know that the weather is changing. "The climate," as good citizens say. That it rains when it shouldn't, that it's dry when it shouldn't be. And so on. You know that planting dates can no longer be chosen as they were before, because the weather calendar is crooked, changed. But not only that. We also see that the behaviour of the animals has changed: they appear in areas that are not their habitat and in seasons that are not theirs. Here and in the geographies of our sister peoples, there is an increase in what are called "natural disasters," but which in fact are a consequence of what the dominant system, that is, capitalism, does and does not do. There are rains, as usual, but now they are fiercer and in places and seasons that are not the same as before. There are terrible droughts. And now it happens that, in the same geography — for example here in Mexico— on one side there are floods and on the other there is drought, and people run out of water. There are strong winds, as if the wind gets so strong and says "enough is enough" and wants to knock everything down. There are earthquakes, volcanic eruptions and plagues like never before. As if Mother Earth were saying "enough is enough," no more. As if humanity were a disease, a virus that must be expelled by vomiting destruction. But, in addition to the fact that Mother Earth is protesting violently, the worst thing is the monster, the Hydra, capitalism, which is like a madman stealing and destroying everything. Now it wants to steal what it did not care about before, and to continue destroying the little of anything that is left. (EZLN, 2023a)

However, the Zapatista ontology that is intrinsic to the proposition of a "communal territory" is a call to the capacity of peoples to place the defence of life at the centre of their existence, as a communal utopia to be built collectively, in other words, as a communitarian political commitment based on territorial belonging. By evoking the vitality that sustains our existence, *altsil* (everything lives), they activate an ontological understanding of time: the temporality of nature and our existence with it is not the same as the temporality of capital. The construction of the commons does not pass through the prism of capital or the legal recognition of the state. On the contrary, building the commons means constructing new social relations in which we recognize ourselves in common in the daily confrontation of contradictions but also in our utopias. And in the Zapatista utopia, the defence of existence is an ontological paradigm in which the commons cannot be appropriated.

We cannot lose sight of the fact that the construction of a communal territory depends on a permanent process of political organization and on the reinvigoration of the forms of socio-cultural, spiritual and political life that are typical of non-capitalist societies. The Zapatista autonomous territories are a contemporary form of these societies, and the reflections made here are aimed not only at understanding their struggle for territorial autonomy but also at seeing what their struggle can inspire in other experiences of resistance to ontocide and to capital's onslaught of dispossession.

Communal territory does not allude to private property, or even collective property, because it is everyone's territory; it is "non-property," or it is a territory of nature and not of humans. It is in the logic of capitalism and colonization that the denomination of private property was established for the people of a certain social class. What we have tried to do in these lines is reflect on the radical critique of private property, which of course is the genesis of Marx's original accumulation. The expanded reproduction of capital is also sustained, in contemporary trade treaties, by a discourse, a false narrative, of trade and commerce for the so-called "common good," of "development" for the common good. It is essential to break with this discourse of the totalization of the commons for the benefit of capital.

On the other hand, in the light of Zapatista political praxis, the call to build "communal territory" is linked to the idea of emancipation as a collective and long-term project, which challenges us to break away from the immediacy intrinsic to capitalist rationality. Territories for life are erected in another temporality, specific to the experiential ontology of *o'tán-puy* or *o'tán-tot*, at the heart of the multiple meanings attributed to the ancestral experience of the community social fabric in its coexistence with the territory. In the case of Zapatismo, there is a conceptual corpus that underpins intersubjective relations and the meanings attributed to coexistence with nature, in the recognition that there is a vital existence, an *altzil* — an everything lives.

In one communiqué, the Zapatistas refer to the little girl Dení, who will be born in the future and that her existence will depend on the commitment we make in the present to stop the destruction by capital: "Therefore, we have to fight so that this child, who will be born in 120 years' time, will be free" (EZLN, 2023a). It is essential to activate the collective *ch'ulel* in defence of life, in the understanding of a "territorial we" that defines our coexistence as interrelated beings. The common is created in a communal social world that will not necessarily be experienced by us, but by future generations. And the future is ancestral, as the Krenak indigenous people of Brazil teach us (Krenak, 2024).

Notes

1   The Zapatista Little School – First Level – Freedom According to the Zapatistas was held in the week following the commemorations of the tenth anniversary of the *caracoles* and the JBGs, August 11–16, December 25–30, 2013, and January 3–7, 2014. The Zapatista School was an invitation for Mexican and international civil society to spend a week in the Zapatista territories to learn about the achievements, advances, limits and challenges of autonomy, within the framework of twenty years of the armed uprising and ten years of consolidation of the Zapatista *caracoles*. The participants stayed with a Zapatista family, were accompanied by a *votán* (something like a political and spiritual guide) and participated in activities with the family and the community. They also received a set of four books on autonomous self-government and Zapatista resistance.

2   Held May 3–5, 2015, at CIDECI, in San Cristóbal de las Casas, Chiapas. All the presentations of the Zapatistas and invited guests were published in a three-volume anthology the same year.

3   A reflection present in the intellectual production of José Carlos Mariátegui, though demarcated as a Peruvian problem.

4   Many of the EZLN communiqués are translated into English and several other languages, and these translations are available as links on their web page.

5   As presented in this book, the EZLN emphasize the importance of reading Marxist and revolutionary theory.

6   To learn more about other concepts, we suggest reading: Lenkersdorf (2005; 2002); López Intzín (2013); Paoli (2003).

7   "Below and on the left, where the heart lies," is a Zapatista slogan that is a play on words. Of course the heart in below and to the left in relation to the human head, but "below" also refers to the poor, to the working class and peasants, and to the left, also refers to the political spectrum.

8   Organized by the Zapatista Movement and open to the public, it took place in December 2014 at CIDECI, San Cristóbal de las Casas, Chiapas.

9   During the First World Festival of Resistances and Rebellions against Capitalism, held in 2014, at CIDECI, San Cristóbal de las Casas, Chiapas.

Radical, Popular, Peoples', Communitarian and Class Autonomy

A decade after the Zapatista uprising, Araceli Burguete Cal y Mayor (2005) contrasted *de facto,* radical autonomies with *de jure* autonomies, that is, legally recognized autonomies. A scholar of the processes of autonomy in Mexico, Burguete Cal y Mayor points out that *de facto* autonomies are forms of indigenous resistance that challenge the state and question the legitimacy and legality of its institutions. In this case the Zapatistas took the decision to break with the legal order of the Mexican state and to build their own institutions. Zapatismo, then, is an emblematic expression of *de facto* autonomy.

If one compares Zapatista autonomy with legal autonomies in Latin America, one notices the weaknesses of the latter in terms of co-optation and demobilization (González, 2010) as opposed to the obvious radicalism of the former. However, there is another comparison that is worthwhile to make. Like most legal autonomies (with a few exceptions, such as the Peasant Reserve Zones in Colombia), most of the other proposals that could be called "radical" are (mono-)ethnic in nature. Such is the case of the Coordinadora Arauco-Malleco (CAM), an armed autonomous movement in Chile, which claims Mapuche autonomy (CAM, 2022). This always leads to the question: what will happen to "subaltern" ethnicities within autonomous regions "governed" by a different "subaltern" ethnicity? This was the basis of the differences between the Confederation of Indigenous Nationalities of Ecuador (CONAIE) and the National Confederation of Peasant, Indigenous and Black Organizations (FENOCIN) in debates a few years ago between the *plurinationality* (the state divided into ethnic nations) of the CONAIE and the proposal of *interculturality* of FENOCIN (territories shared among peasants, indigenous peoples and African-descended peoples), as explained by Philipp Altmann (2013). On the other hand, although the EZLN is an indigenous movement, in the sense that it has a vast majority Mayan base, its radical autonomy is not ethnic; it is more of a popular, communitarian or class base. There are no Tzotzil or Chole *caracoles,* but rather regional self-governments that represent and govern all those who live there and who recognize and identify with Zapatista autonomy.

The cultural and political experience of Zapatismo highlights the tran-
scendence of the community, situating it as a social structure of complex
organizational and political connections. The community as a space for
the daily construction of politics and the political reveals a resistance that
has its origin in a social reproduction framed in colonial and neocolonial
contexts. In this direction, thinkers such as José Carlos Mariátegui and, in
contemporary social theory, González Casanova, recognize the revolutionary power of native peoples:

> Indians transform their community into a social structure
> prepared to resist the long colonial war. The Indian community
> is much more than a refuge. It is the social basis for production,
> trade, migration, rebellion and politics ... the internal structure of
> the Indian community contributes to understanding its strength.
> (González Casanova, 2009a, p. 293)

The indigenous community and its political force were transmuted
into the creation of the Zapatista *caracoles* and good government councils,
a new way of thinking and waging political struggle based on networks of
resistance and autonomy (González Casanova, 2003). The organizational
structure of the Zapatista autonomous municipalities, with autonomous
governments and collective works, opened the way to imagining another
conception of politics, of democracy, in consonance with the "people," the
historical subject of Latin American and Caribbean revolutionary discourse,
who should take the struggles for liberation and emancipation into their
own hands (Starr et al., 2011).

Inspired by the Zapatista autonomic project, González Casanova (2003)
argues that autonomy constitutes a path of opposition to the logics of power
framed in a state-centric perspective, that is, in the "power of the state,"
typical of both "revolutionary" and reformist positions. He considers that
the political experience of the Zapatista *caracoles* represents the collective
will to build a democratic process erected in the articulation of "peoples-
governments" and that it should be thought of as a concrete example of true
grassroots democracy, in which the people occupy their place as historical
subjects in consolidation of people's power:

> They combine and integrate in practice both logics, that of the
> construction of power by networks of autonomous peoples and
> the integration of organs of power as self-governments of those
> who fight for an alternative within the system .... The *caracoles*
> correspond to a new style of exercising the power of communities

enmeshed in resistance and for resistance, in which their co-mandantes submit to the communities, to build and follow the lines of struggle and organization, without ceasing to offer "their word," though always with respect for the autonomy and dignity of individuals and peoples. (2009a, p. 339)

The community framework takes on centrality because it represents the historical accumulation of a resistance of more than five centuries and that has not been encapsulated in the homogenizing logic of capitalism and its politics that ultimately denies power to the people (Barkin and Sánchez, 2019). In this direction, the political praxis of Zapatismo inspires us, above all, in the conceptual expansion of the revolutionary subject, always present in the Latin American and Caribbean theoretical and political tradition, elaborating upon historical and sociological interpretations of "liberation," constantly asking ourselves what are the paths to build as communities that have resisted the oppressors since the long night of 500 years.

The armed insurgency of an indigenous army and autonomy as a grass-roots political process, of "peoples-governments," constitute a new-old horizon for the exercise of "democracy by all and for all," linked to the rethinking of the political struggle and to the recovery of other ways of organization of life and political activity from prior to Western frameworks of a colonial and capitalist character. Autonomy, conceived and implemented from the perspective of indigenous peoples, consolidates a renewal in the conception of a popular political project and a democracy of and for the peoples.

In the crucible of the popular struggles around the turn of the century, those carried out by indigenous movements, either in direct dispute with the state, or in the interpellation of the form of the state, as in the case of Zapatismo, challenge us to engage in a collective theoretical-analytical revision, within the frameworks of political and social sciences. In the realm of critical theory, they instigate us to imagine a historical-political subject forged in a millenary resistance and what this means in the updating of a sociology of emancipation. Moved by the same feeling, González Casanova argues:

In rebellious peoples like the Zapatistas, we do not see a merely indigenous rebellion, which would be very legitimate. We see the only force that, coming from the poor of the earth, is potentially capable of creating or building an alternative world in which the struggles for freedom, justice and democracy are made concrete, that is, for the various projects of the emancipation of human beings and the protection of Nature and life on Earth. (2009b, p. 308)

What more can be said about Zapatismo, its autonomy and its teachings? We say *a lot,* but in the format of this small book, one of a series of small books, we do not have the space to present the many other aspects of Zapatista autonomy (like autonomous health, autonomous justice, agrarian reform-recovered land, autonomous communications, etc.) nor to further detail the myriad key moments in the Zapatista timeline. These include how Zapatismo helped inaugurate an end-of-the-century-turn-of-the-century era of anti-globalization mobilizations and World Social Forums, called the Movement of Movements (Rosset, Martínez-Torres and Hernández Navarro, 2005); the counterinsurgency carried out by the "bad governments," the current siege by the drug cartels and the new-old paramilitary groups, and the independent candidacy for the presidency of the country (Fuentes Sánchez, 2022); and the complicated situation of Zapatismo and indigenous peoples during the so-called progressive governments of the Morena Party in Mexico (López and Rivas, 2020). However, we hope that this book inspires our readers to seek more information on the Zapatista theme. There is a vast neo-Zapatista literature, so large that in this small book we cannot do justice to or include many important authors. What we have tried to do is to outline some of the most important elements and lessons of Zapatista history, of its thought and development processes and its contributions to critical theory and to the study of social movements and of the autonomies that movements often build. To paraphrase the great Filipino scholar of agrarian issues, Saturnino (Jun) Borras Jr., we leave you with this "small book that tries to summarize in a few pages the state of the art of a large subject."

Postscript to the English Language Edition

Note from the authors:

In late 2023, after the orginal Spanish-language manuscript for this book was finished, the Zapatistas published a series of highly significant communiques, in which, among things, they dissolved the regional good government councils (JBGs) and autonomous rebel municipalities (MAREZ), which are referred to throughout this book, replacing them with new structures. Among the new structures, as explained in Part 1 which follows, are local autonomous governments (GALs), collectives of Zapatista autonomous governments (CGAZs) and assemblies of collectives of Zapatista autonomous governments (ACGAZs). The new structure was created in order to both confront the new reality that indigenous communities in Chiapas, in which both Zapatista and non-Zapatista, are under (apparently government sanctioned) siege by armed drug cartels, and to address certain defects of the previous structures, which are outlined in Part 2. These new structures are also complemented by the new figure of "communal territory," which we analyze at the end of this book and which was announced in the communique reproduced here in Part 3. This three-part postscript is essential reading for anyone who wishes to understand Zapatismo as a living movement in permanent evolution.

Part 1: The New Structure of Zapatista Autonomy

November 2023

Brothers, sisters, comrades:

I am going to try to explain to you how we reorganized the autonomy, that is, the new structure of the Zapatista autonomy. I will explain more to you later in more detail. Or maybe I won't explain more, because practice is what matters. Of course you can also come to the anniversary and watch the plays, songs, poems and the art and culture of this new stage of our struggle. If not, Tercios Compas will send you photos and videos. At another time I will tell you what we saw that was good and bad in the critical evaluation of MAREZ and JBG. Now I'll just tell you how it looks. Here it goes:

First: The main base, which is not only where autonomy is sustained, also without which the other structures cannot function, is the Local Autonomous Government [GAL for its acronym in Spanish]. There is a GAL in each community where Zapatista support bases live. The Zapatista GALs are the core and foundation of all autonomy. They are coordinated by autonomous agents and commissioners and are subject to the assembly of the town, ranchería, community, area, neighborhood, ejido, colony, or however each population calls itself. Each GAL controls its autonomous organizational resources (such as schools and clinics) and the relationship with neighboring non-Zapatista sister towns. And controls the proper use of money. It also detects and reports mismanagement, corruption and errors that may exist. And is attentive to those who want to pass themselves off as Zapatista authorities to ask for support or aid that they use for their own benefit.

So, if before there were a few dozen Zapatista Rebel Autonomous Municipalities — MAREZs — now there are thousands of Zapatista GALs.

Second: According to their needs, problems and advances, various GALs are convened into Collectives of Zapatista Autonomous Government [CGAZ for its acronym in Spanish], and here discussions are held and agreements are made on matters that interest the convening GALs. When they so determine, the Collective of Autonomous Governments calls an assembly of the authorities of each community. Here the plans and needs of Health, Education, Agroecology, Justice, Commerce, and those that are needed are proposed, discussed and approved or rejected. The coordinators of each area are at the CGAZ level. They are not authorities. Their job is to coordinate the work requested by the GAL or that are deemed necessary for community life. Such as, for example: preventive medicine and vaccination campaigns, campaigns for endemic diseases, courses and specialized training (such as laboratory technicians, x rays, ultrasound, mammograms and those that we learn on the way), literacy and higher levels, sporting and cultural events, traditional festivities, etc. Each region or CGAZ has its coordinators, who are the ones who summon assemblies if there is an urgent problem or one that affects several communities.

That is to say, where before there were 12 Good Government 'Juntas', now there will be hundreds.

Third: Next, the Assemblies of Collectives of Zapatista Autonomous Governments [ACGAZ for its acronym in Spanish]. Which are what were previously known as zones. But they have no authority and depend on the CGAZ. And the CGAZ depend on the GAL. The ACGAZ convenes and presides over zone assemblies, when necessary according to the requests of

GAL and CGAZ. They are based in the caracoles but move between regions. In other words, they are mobile, according to the towns' demands for attention.

Fourth: As will be seen in practice, the Command and Coordination of Autonomy has been transferred from the JBG and MAREZ to the towns and communities, to the GAL. The zones (ACGAZ) and the regions (CGAZ) are governed by the towns, they must be accountable to the towns and must find a way to meet their needs in Health, Education, Justice, Food and those that arise due to emergencies caused by natural disasters, pandemics, crimes, invasions, wars, and the other misfortunes that the capitalist system brings.

Fifth: The structure and disposition of the EZLN has been reorganized in order to increase the defense and security of towns and mother earth in the event of aggressions, attacks, epidemics, invasion of companies that prey on nature, partial or total military occupations, natural catastrophes and nuclear wars. We have prepared so that our towns survive, even isolated from each other.

Sixth: We understand that you may have problems assimilating this. And that, for a while, you will struggle to understand it. It took us 10 years to think about it, and of those 10 years, 3 to prepare it for its practice.

We also understand that it seems to you that your thinking is scrambled. That is why it is necessary to change your channel of understanding. Only by looking far away, backwards and forwards, can the present step be understood.

We hope you understand that it is a new structure of autonomy, that we are just learning and that it will take a while to get going well.

In reality, this statement has only the intention of telling you that Zapatista autonomy continues and advances, that we think it will be better for the towns, communities, places, neighborhoods, colonies, ejidos and rancherías where they live, that is, the bases of Zapatista support. And that it has been their decision, taking into account their ideas and proposals, their criticisms and self-criticisms.

Also, as will be seen, this new stage of autonomy is made to confront the worst of the Hydra, its most infamous bestiality and its destructive madness. Their wars and business and military invasions.

For us, there are no borders or distant geographies. Everything that happens in any corner of the planet affects us and concerns us, worries us and hurts us. To the extent of our very small strength, we will support human beings in distress regardless of their color, race, nationality, belief, ideology and language. Although we do not know many languages or understand many cultures and ways, we know how to understand the suffering, pain, sorrow, and proud rage that the system provokes.

We know how to read and listen to brother hearts. We will continue trying to learn from them, their stories and their struggles. Not only because we have suffered from this for centuries and we know what it is like. Also, and above all because, as for 30 years, our fight is for life.

Surely we have made many mistakes in all these years. We will surely do more in the next 120 years. But we will NOT give up, we will NOT change path, we will NOT sell out. We will always be reviewing our struggle, its times and ways with a critical eye.

Our eyes, our ears, our heads and our hearts will always be ready to learn from others who, although different in many things, have our same concerns and similar desires for democracy, freedom and justice.

And we will always seek the best for our people and for our sister communities.

We are, therefore, Zapatistas.

As long as there is at least one man, one woman, one 'otroa' Zapatista in any corner of the planet, we will resist in rebellion, that is, we will fight.

See it for yourselves, friends and enemies. And those who are neither one thing nor another.

That is it, for now.

From the mountains of the Mexican southeast.

— Insurgent Subcommander Moisés.

Mexico, November 2023

More than 500, 40, 30, 20, 10 years later.

P.S. Here I leave you a drawing to see if you understand it a little. (EZLN 2023a)

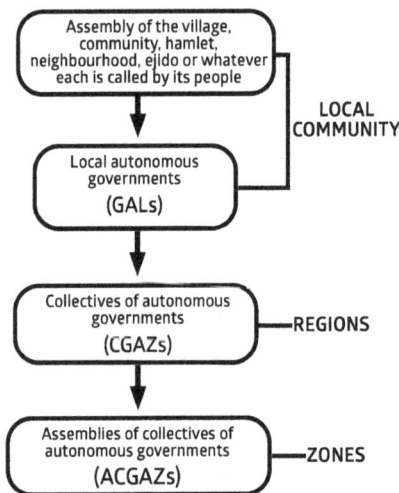

Part 2: Regarding Pyramids and Their Uses and Customary Regimes

Conclusions from the critical analysis of MAREZ and JBG. (Fragment of an interview with Subcomandante Insurgente Moisés during the months of August-September 2023, in the mountains of Southeast Mexico)

November 2023
Introduction

> *Who built Thebes of the 7 gates? In the books you will read*
>
> *the names of kings. Did the kings haul up the lumps of rock?*
>
> *And Babylon, many times demolished, who raised it up so many times?*
>
> *In what houses of gold glittering Lima did its builders live? Where,*
>
> *the evening that the Great Wall of China was finished, did the masons go?*
>
> *Great Rome is full of triumphal arches. Who erected them?*
>
> — Bertold Brecht

Known is the obsession that dominant systems have, throughout their history, in rescuing the image of the defeated dominant classes or castes. As if in the winner inhabited the worry of neutralizing the image of the defeated: avoiding his fall. In the study of the remains of the defeated civilization or culture, emphasis is usually placed on the great palaces of the rulers, the religious buildings of the high hierarchy, and the statues or monuments that the dominant people of that time made of themselves.

Not always studied with genuine anthropological or archeological interest (it is not the same thing) are the Pyramids, for example, studied. The architectural-religious sense — sometimes also scientific — and what tourist brochures (and political programs across the spectrum) call "the splendor of the past."

It is natural that the different governments take notice and, not without longing sighs, concentrate on kings and queens. The great palaces and pyramids can be pointed out as references of the scientific advance of those times, of the social organization and of the causes "of its development and decline," but no ruler likes to see his future reflected in the past. That is why they twist past history, and it is possible to reschedule foundations of cities, empires and "transformations." So, without realizing it, every *selfie* taken at archaeological sites hides more than what it shows. Up there, the winner of today will be the defeated of tomorrow.

But, if there are no mentions about these constructions having someone who designed them — their architects, engineers and artists — there will be even fewer references to "the labor force," that is, to the men and women on whose backs (in more than a sense) were built the wonders that amaze tourists from all over the world, while they make time to go to the club, the mall and the beach.

From that point to ignoring that the descendants of that "labor force" remain alive and active, with language and culture, there is only one step. The natives who built, for example, the pyramids of Teotihuacán and the Mayan area in the Mexican southeast, exist (that is, resist) and, sometimes, they add to their resistance that subversive component that is rebellion.

In the case of Mexico, the different governments prefer the natives as living crafts and, sometimes, as choreography ad hoc. The current government does not represent any change in this (well, not only in that, but that is not the point). Native peoples continue to be objects of alms (that aspirin for scoundrels), mobilization of the vote, artisanal curiosity and a vanishing point for those who administer the ongoing destruction: "I am going to destroy your life, that is, your territory; but don't worry, I'm going to preserve the pyramids of those who exploited your ancestors and those funny things you say, and dress and do."

Having said this, this "image" of the pyramid — the narrow upper tip and the wide lower base — is now used by Subcomandante Insurgente Moisés to explain to us something of what was the analysis (ferocious and implacable, in my opinion) of the work of the MAREZ and Good Government Juntas.

—The Captain[1]

Some history, not much, just 30 years

The MAREZ and Good Government Juntas were not all bad. We must remember how we got to them. For the Zapatista towns they were like a school of political literacy. A self-literacy.

Most of us did not know how to read, write, or speak Spanish. Furthermore, we spoke different languages. That was good, because then our idea and our practice did not come from outside, but rather we had to search in our heads, in our history as indigenous people, in our own way.

We had never had the opportunity to govern ourselves. We were always governed. Even before the Spanish, the Aztec empire, which the current government loves very much — I think because they like bossy people — oppressed many languages and cultures. Not only in what is now Mexico, also in what is now Central America.

The situation we were in was one of death and despair. They closed everything to us. There were no doors, no windows, no cracks. As if they wanted us to drown. So, as they say, we had to open a crack in that wall that enclosed us and condemned us. As if everything were darkness and with our blood we lit a little light. That was the Zapatista uprising, a little light in the darkest night.

Then it came that many people asked for a ceasefire, that we had to talk. The citizens already know about that. The same thing had happened to many of them as to us, that bad governments never fulfilled their word. And they do not comply because governments are the main oppressors. So we had to choose if we hope and wait that one day they comply, or if we look for a solution on our own. And we chose to find our way.

And well, you had to organize for that. We had organized and prepared for 10 years to take up arms, to die and kill. And then it turns out that we had to organize ourselves to live. And living is freedom. And justice. And to be able to govern ourselves as people, not as little children which is the way governments see us.

That's where it got into our heads that we have to make a government that obeys. In other words, that it did not do as it pleased, but rather, did what the people say. In other words, "command by obeying," which are the words that today's scoundrels plagiarize (*in other words, they do not only plagiarize theses. Editorial note*).

So with the autonomous municipalities we learned that we can govern ourselves. And that was possible because many people supported us, without any interest, to find the path of life. In other words, those people did not come to see what they could get — like those that I imagine you are going to tell outsiders when you talk about 30 years — but rather they really committed themselves to a life project. And there were those who wanted to tell us how we should do it. But we did not take up arms to change the boss. There is no good boss. But there were other people who did respect our thoughts, our way.

The value of the word

When we obtain that support, it is like a commitment that we make. If we say that we need support to create schools and clinics, to prepare health and education promoters, to give an example, then we have to comply. In other words, we cannot say that it is for one thing and use it for another. We had then and have now to be honest, because these people do not come to exploit us, but to encourage us. That's how we saw it.

So we have to put up with the attacks and the bullshit from the bad governments, from the landowners, from the big companies, who are trying hard to test us to see if we can endure it or it is easy for us to fall into a provocation so they are able to accuse us of telling lies, that we also want power and pay. And the thing about power is that it is like a disease that kills good ideas and corrupts, that is, it makes people sick. And there you have a person who seems like a good person, well, with power, he goes crazy. Or maybe he was already crazy and power sort of stripped naked his heart.

So we think that we need to organize, for example, our health. Because of course we saw and see that what the government does is a big lie that is only to steal and does not care that people die, especially if they are indigenous.

And it happened that, when we make that crack in the system and look out, we see many things. But also many people see us. And among those people, there are those who looked at us and took the risk of helping and supporting us. Because what if we are liars and don't do what we say? But hey, they took a risk and they committed [to] us.

Look, out there, in the cities, giving your word is no good. They can say one thing in one moment, and a minute later they say the opposite and is as if nothing had happened, all is calm. There is, for example, what they call "mañanera," that one day they say one thing and another day the opposite. But, as it pays, they applaud him and are happy because he gives them alms that do not even come from his work, but from what working people give to governments with taxes, which are like the protection racket of disorganized crime.

So those people support us and we start little by little with preventive medicine. Since we had already recovered the lands, we improved our diet, but more was needed. So, health. We must recover herbal knowledge, but it is not enough, science is also needed. And thanks to doctors, that we call "fraternities" because they are like our brothers, who got on board and guided us. So the first Health trainers were born or formed, that is, those who prepare the promoters.

And also education, especially Castilian. Because for us Spanish is very important because it is like the bridge through which we can communicate and understand each other between different languages. For example, if you speak Tzeltal, you are going to struggle to communicate with the Cho'ol language, or Tzotzil, or Tojolabal, or Zoque, or Mame, or Quiché. So, you have to learn Spanish. And autonomous schools are very important for that. For example, our generation speaks combined mother tongues and Spanish, that is, not all well, that is, we speak crooked. But there are already generations of young people, who learned in autonomous schools, who know Castilian better than some citizens. The late Sup Marcos said that these young people could correct the writings of university students. And you know that, before, to make a complaint, you had to go to the Command to write it. But then not anymore. In each autonomous authority there was one writer, and well, it worked.

Then it is like one advancement kind of pushes another. And soon after, these young people want more, to learn more. So we organize our health in each town, each region and zone. We are advancing in each area of health, midwives, medicinal plants, orthopedics, laboratories, dentists, ultrasound, among other areas, there are clinics. And the same in school, that is, education. We say school, because we adults also lack education, it is very broad for us, education, and not just children and adolescents.

Furthermore, we organized productive work because we already had land, which was previously in the hands of landowners. And so we work as a family and as a collective in the cornfield, the bean fields, the coffee fields, vegetables, and farms. And some livestock, which is used more for economic emergencies and for holidays. The collective work allowed the economic independence of women comrades and that brought many more things. But they have already talked about that.

A school

In other words, we learned to govern ourselves and thus we were able to put aside bad governments and organizations that say they are leftist, progressive and I don't know what else. 30 years learning what it means to be autonomous, that is, we direct ourselves, we govern ourselves. And it has not been easy, because all the governments that have passed from PRI, PAN, PRD, PT, VERDE and MORENA, their desire to destroy us does not end. For this reason, just as in past governments, in this one they say that we have already disappeared, or that we have already fled, or that we are already very defeated, or that there is no longer any Zapatista, that we went to the United States or Guatemala. But you see, well here we are. In resistance and rebellion.

And the most important thing we learned in the MAREZ is that autonomy is not about theory, about writing books and making speeches. It is something that needs to be done. And we have to do it as towns and not wait for someone to come and do it for us.

All of this is, let's say, the good thing about MAREZ: a school of practical autonomy.

And the Good Government Juntas were also very important because with them we learned to exchange ideas about struggles with other brothers from Mexico and the world, where we saw it [was] right, we took it, and where we saw it was not, we discarded it. Some tell us that we have to obey just as they say. Where is that going to happen? If we put our lives at stake. In other words, that is what we are worth: our blood and that of generations that came before and those to come. We are not here for anyone to come and tell us what we are going to do, even if they say that they are very knowledgeable. With the JBG we learned to meet and organize, to think, to give an opinion, to propose, to discuss, to study, to analyze and to decide for ourselves.

So, as a summary, I tell you that the MAREZ and JBG helped us learn that theory without practice is pure words. And practice without theory, well it is as if you walked like a blind man. And since there is no theory of what we started to do, that is, there is no manual or book, then we have also had to make our own theory. We stumbled through theory and practice. I think that's why the theorists and the revolutionary vanguards don't like us very much, because we didn't just take away their jobs. We also showed them that talking is one thing and reality is another. And here we are, the ignorant and backwards, as they call us, the ones who cannot find the way because we are peasants. But here we are and even if they deny us, we exist. Too bad.

The Pyramid

Well, now it's time for the bad things. Or rather not bad, but it proved that it will no longer be useful for what is to come. In addition to the inherent flaws. As you tell me, we will talk later about how all of this started, about how it got into our heads, we'll see it later.

The main problem is the damn pyramid. The pyramid separated the authorities from the towns, they distanced themselves between towns and authorities. The proposals from authorities did not go down as they were to the people, nor do the opinions of the people reach the authorities.

Because of the pyramid, a lot of information is cut, the guidelines, suggestions, support of ideas that the CCRI comrades explain. The Good Government Junta does not fully transmit, and the same thing happens when things are explained to the Authorities of the Zapatista Rebel Autonomous Municipalities, the same again is repeated when the MAREZ inform the assemblies of authorities of towns, and finally this is what happens with the authorities of the towns when they explain to each town. Many cuts of information or interpretations, or additions that were not there originally.

And many efforts were also made in the training of authorities and every 3 years new ones leave and enter. And the main base of village authorities is not being prepared. In other words, no relays were formed. "Government collective" we said and it was not fully fulfilled, the work was rarely done this way and the greater part what [was?] not fulfilled, both in MAREZ and in the JBG.

It was already falling into wanting to decide themselves, the authorities, the tasks and the decisions, as in MAREZ and JBG. They wanted to leave aside the 7 principles of commanding by obeying.

There were also NGOs, who forcefully want the projects that they had in the JBG and the MAREZ to be accepted but they are not what the people needed. And people who visited remain friends of a family or a town and they only sent some help to them. And some visitors outright wanted to direct us and treat us like their waiters. And so with great kindness we had to remind them that we are Zapatistas.

And there was also, in some MAREZ and JBG, poor administration of people's resources, and, of course, they were sanctioned.

In other words, in summary, it was seen that the structure of how we were governed, as a pyramid, was not the way. It's not from below, it's from above.

If Zapatismo were only the EZLN, it is easy to give orders. But the government must be civil, not military. Then the people have to find their way, their way and their time. Where and when to do what. The military should be only for defense. Pyramid may be useful for military purposes, but not for civilian purposes. That's what we see.

On another occasion we will tell what the situation is here in Chiapas. But now we just say that it is like anywhere else. It is worse than last years. Now they kill them in their homes, in their streets, in their towns. And there is no government that sees and listens to the demands of the people. And they don't do anything because they themselves are the criminals.

Not only that. We have already said that we see many misfortunes that are going to arrive or that are already here. If you see that it is going to rain or that the first drops are already falling and the sky is black as a politician's soul, then you take out your poncho and look for where you are going to go. The problem is that there is nowhere to protect yourself. You have to build your own shelter.

The thing is that we saw that with MAREZ and JBG we will not be able to face the storm. We need Deni to grow and live and for all the other seven generations to be born and live.

For all this and the rest, we entered into a great series of reflections and came to the conclusion that we only have left a great discussion of all the towns and analysis, of how to face the new and bad situation and at the same time how we are going to continue to govern us. Meetings and assemblies were held, area by area, until an agreement was reached that there would no longer be Good Government Juntas or Zapatista Rebel Autonomous Municipalities. And that we need a new structure, that is, to accommodate ourselves in another way.

Of course, this proposal is not just about reorganizing. It is also a new initiative. A new challenge. But I think that's what we'll say later.

So in general, without much fuss, then, the MAREZ and JBG were very useful at that stage. But another step follows, and those clothes are already too small for us, and they break and even though you mend them, it's for nothing. Because there will come a time when you're left with pure rags.

So what we did is cut the pyramid. So we cut it from the tip. Or rather, we turned it upside down.

Do we celebrate the past or the future?

We have to keep walking and in the middle of the storm. But we as towns are already used to walking with everything against us.

This coming December and January, we do not celebrate the 30 years of the uprising. For us every day is a celebration, because we are alive and fighting.

We will celebrate that we began a path that will take us at least 120 years, maybe more. We've been rolling for more than 500 years, so it won't be long, just over a century. And that is no longer so far away. It is, as José Alfredo Jiménez says, "just there behind that hill."

From the mountains of the Mexican Southeast.

—Subcomandante Insurgente Moisés

(Fragment of the interview conducted by Captain Marcos, for the Tercios Compas. Copyleft Mexico, November 2023. Authorization of the JBG … ah wow, if there are no more Juntas … well, of the MAREZ … well, neither … Well, the thing is that it is authorized. The interview was conducted the old-fashioned way, that is, like reporters used to do, with a notebook and pen. Now they don't even go to the place to look for the note, they take it from social networks. Yes, a shame, my man).

I attest.

—The Captain, dancing to the cumbia "Sopa de caracol."

Dance! No matter if there's mud!

Part 3: The Common and Non-Property

"Open wide your eyes, son, and follow the Pujuy bird. He is not wrong. His destiny is like ours: to walk so that others do not get lost."

—Canek, Ermilo Abreu Gómez

On some past occasion, a few years ago, the Zapatista people explained to themselves the struggle "as the women that we are" pointing out, not a matter of mere will, disposition or study, but the material basis that made this change possible: the economic independence of Zapatista women. And they were not referring to having a job and salary or the alms in coins with which governments across the political spectrum buy votes and memberships. They pointed to collective work as the fertile ground for this change. That is, organized work that was not intended for individual well-being, but for that of the group. It was not just about getting together for crafts, commerce, raising livestock, or planting and harvesting corn, coffee, and vegetables. Also, and, perhaps, above all, it was about their own spaces, without men. Imagine what in those times and places they spoke and speak among themselves: their pain, their anger, their ideas, their proposals, their dreams.

I will not go into more detail about it — the compañeras have their own voice, history and destiny. I only mention it because it remains to be known what is the material base on which the new stage that the Zapatista communities have decided will be built. The new initiative, as outsiders would classify it.

I am proud to point out that not only was the entire proposal the product, from its very conception, of the Zapatista organizational leadership collective- all of it of indigenous blood with Mayan roots. Also, that my work was limited to providing information that my bosses "crossed" with their own, and, later, to look for and argue objections and probable future failures (the aforementioned "hypothesis" to which I referred in a previous text). In the end, when they finished their deliberation and they specified the central idea, to submit it for consultation with all the peoples, I was as surprised as perhaps you will be now that you are going to know about it.

In this other fragment of the interview with Subcomandante Insurgente Moisés, he explains to us how they came to this idea of "the common." Perhaps some of you can appreciate the deeply rebellious and subversive meaning of this in which, for the same reason, we risk our existence.

—The Captain

Non-Ownership

Well, in summary this is our proposal: to establish large areas of recovered land as common. That is, without property. Neither private, nor ejidal, nor communal, nor federal, nor state, nor business, nor anything. A non-ownership of land. As they say: "land without papers." So, in those lands that are going to be defined, if they ask who owns that land or who is the owner, the answer will be: "nobody's," that is, they are "common."

If you ask if it is the land of Zapatistas, or 'partidistas' or who, well, none of them. Or all of them, it's the same. There is no commissioner or agent to buy, kill, disappear. What there is, is people who work and take care of those lands. And they defend them.

An important part is that, in order for this to be achieved, there has to be an agreement between the residents regardless of whether they are 'partidistas' [non-Zapatistas who support one or another political party] or Zapatistas. In other words, they have to talk between themselves, not to bad governments. Seeking permission from bad governments has only brought divisions and even deaths among peasants themselves.

So, respecting the lands that are individual-family property, and those that are for collective works, this non-ownership is created on land recovered in these years of war. And it is proposed that it is worked together in shifts, regardless of what party you are, or what religion, or what color, or what size, or what gender you are.

The rules are simple: it has to be an agreement between the residents of a region. Do not grow drugs, do not sell the land, do not allow the entry of any company or industry. Paramilitaries are excluded. The product of the work of those lands belongs to those who work it in the agreed time. There are no taxes, nor payment of tithes. Each facility that is built is left for the next group. They take only the product of their work. But we will talk more about all this later.

This, very summarized, is what was presented and consulted with all the Zapatista villages. And it turned out that the vast majority agreed. And also that, in some Zapatista regions, it had already been done for years.

And what we did was, well, propose a path to weather the storm and reach the other side safely. And not to take that path alone as Zapatistas, but together as the indigenous peoples that we are. Of course, more will come out about this proposal: about health, about education, about justice, about government, about life. Let's say that we see this as necessary to be able to face the storm.

To Think the Path and the Step

How did it get into our heads? Well, I'll tell you. We saw several things. So this idea didn't just come out all at once. As if they came together and as if we saw it part by part and then everything together.

One was the storm. Everything that refers to the unconformity of nature. Its way of protesting, increasingly louder and increasingly terrible. Because we say destruction, but many times what happens is that nature kind of recovers a place. Or that it attacks invasions of the system: dams, for example. Tourist places, for example, that are built over the death of the coasts. Megaprojects that hurt, injure the earth. So, there comes a response. Sometimes it responds quickly, sometimes it takes a while. And the human being, well, what the system has done with the human being, is as if stunned.

Does not react. Although he sees that misfortune is coming, that there are warnings, that there are alerts, he continues as if nothing had happened and, well, things do happen. They say that such misfortune was surprising. But it turns out that for several years now people have been warning that the destruction of nature is going to take its toll. Science, not us, analyzes it and proves it. We, then, as people of the earth see it. Everything is useless.

Misfortune does not suddenly appear in your house, no. First it gets closer, it makes its noise so you know it is coming. Knocks on your door. Breaks everything. Not only your house, your people, your life, but also your heart. You are no longer calm.

Another thing is what they call social decomposition, or as they say, the social fabric breaks, because of violence. In other words, a community of people is related to certain rules or norms or agreements, as we say. Sometimes written laws are made and sometimes there is nothing written, but nonetheless, people know. In many communities they say "act of agreement" that is, it is put into words. So, it doesn't seem like it's going to get better. What we know is that it will get worse. And that. "This can be done, this cannot be done, this has to be done," and so on. For example, whoever works advances. He who doesn't work stays poor. That it is wrong to force someone to do something that he or she does not want to do, for example, in the case of men against women. That it is wrong to abuse the weak. That it is wrong to kill, steal, rape. But what happens if it's the other way around? If evil is rewarded and goodness is persecuted and punished. For example, an indigenous farmer who sees that the destruction of a forest is wrong, then becomes its guardian. He protects the forest, therefore, from those who destroy it to make a profit. Defending is a good thing, because that brother or sister is taking care of life. That is humane, it is not religious. But it happens that this guardian is persecuted, imprisoned and, not infrequently, murdered. And if you ask what his crime is, why they killed him, and you hear that his crime was defending life, like brother Samir Flores Soberanes, then it is clear that the system is sick, that it no longer has a remedy, that you have to look elsewhere.

What does it take to realize this disease, this rottenness of humanity? You don't need a religion, or a science, or an ideology. Just look, listen, feel.

And then we see that the big bosses, the capitalists, don't care what happens tomorrow. They want to earn money today. As much as possible and as quickly as possible. It doesn't matter if you tell them: "Hey, but what you do destroys and the destruction spreads, grows, becomes uncontrollable and returns to you. As if you were spitting up into the air or urinating against the wind. It comes back to you." And you may think that it is good that misfortune happens to a scoundrel. But it turns out that, before that, it takes away quite a few people who don't even know why. Like babies, for example. What will a child know about religions, ideologies, political parties or whatever. But the system holds those babies responsible. It makes them pay. It destroys in their name, it kills in their name, it lies in their name. And they inherit death and destruction.

Whatever happens, we have to cross the storm and get to the other side. Survive.

Another thing is what we saw on the Journey for Life.[2] What is going on in those parts that are supposed to be more advanced, that are more developed as they say. We saw that all that talk about "Western civilization," "progress" and things like that is a lie. We saw that there was what is necessary for wars and crimes. Now we actually saw two things: one is where the storm is headed if we don't do anything. The other is what other organized rebellions are building in those geographies. In other words, those people look at the same thing that we look at. That is, the storm.

Thanks to these brother peoples we were able to broaden our vision, make it wider. That is, not only look further, but also look at more things. More world, that is.

So we, as indigenous peoples, ask ourselves what will we do, if it is already over, if it is every man for himself. But we see those brothers who act like they don't care what happens to others, that they only look out for themselves, and then it reaches them anyway. They believe they are safe locked inside themselves. But that does not work at all

The Road to Memory

So we think, we remember how it was before. We talked about it to our elders. We asked them if it was like this before. We ask them to tell us if there has always been darkness, death, destruction. Where did that idea of the world come from? How come everything got fucked up. We think that if we know when and how the light, the good thought, the complete knowledge of what is good and what is bad was lost, then maybe we can find that and with that fight for everything to become complete, as it should be, respecting life.

And then we saw how that came to be and we saw that it came with private property. And it is not about changing the name and saying that there is ejidal property or small property or federal property. Because in all cases it is the bad government that gives the papers. In other words, it is the bad government that says if something exists and, with its trick, whether it ceases to exist. As it did with the reform of Salinas de Gortari and with the blows against communal property, which only existed if it was registered and that, with the same laws, they diminish it until it disappears. And communal property, let's say registered, also causes divisions and confrontations. Because those lands legally belong to some, but against others. Property papers do not say "this is yours," what they say is "this is not that person's, attack him."

And there you have the peasants going round and round to be given a piece of paper that says that what is theirs is theirs because they already work for it. And peasants waging war against peasants not even over a piece of land, no, it's over a piece of paper that says who owns that land. And whoever has more papers, well, has more paid support, that is, more deception. Because it turns out that if you have a paper they give you a social program, but they ask you to support, for example, a candidate because that candidate is going to give you the paper and give you money. But it turns out that that same government is deceiving you, because it sells that paper to a company. And then it turns out that the company comes and tells you that you have to leave because that land is not yours because the 'pinche' businessman now has the paper. And you leave either willingly or forcefully. And there they have armies, police and paramilitaries to convince you to leave.

It is enough for the company to say that it wants such land, for the government to decree the expropriation of those lands and tells the company to do its business "for a while." That's what they do with megaprojects.

And all for a 'silly' piece of paper. Although the paper is as old as New Spain, the paper is worthless to the powerful. It's a hoax. It is so that you can trust and be calm until the system discovers that, beneath your poverty, there is oil, gold, uranium, silver. Or that there is a spring of pure water, and now it turns out that water is already a commodity that is bought and sold.

A commodity like your parents, your grandparents, your great-grandparents were. A commodity like you are, and your children, your grandchildren, your great-grandchildren will be, and so on for generations.

So the paper is like the labels of merchandise in the markets, it is the price of the land, of your work, of your descendants. And you don't realize it, but you're already lined up in line at the cashier and you're going to arrive. And it turns out that not only are you going to have to pay, you are also going to leave the store and find that they have taken your merchandise, that you don't even have the paper that you and your ancestors fought so hard for. And that maybe you will leave a paper an as inheritance for your children, and maybe not even that. Government papers are the price of your life, you have to pay that price with your life. So you are a legal commodity. That's the only difference with slavery.

Then the older ones tell you that the problem, the division, the arguments and the fights, came when the property titles arrived. It's not that there weren't problems before, it's that they were resolved by making an agreement.

And the problem is that you can make many papers that split the land many times, but the land does not multiply like the papers. A hectare is still a hectare, even if there are many papers.

Then what happens now with that thing they call 'Fourth Transformation' and its "Sembrando Vida" program: in the ejidos there are the 'rights-holders' — who are the ejidatarios who have the aforementioned paper or agrarian certificate -, and the 'applicants' who, although they participate in the community, they have no paper, because the land is already distributed. Supposedly, the applicants are requesting a piece of land, but in reality, they are requesting a piece of paper that says they are peasants who work the land. So, it is not that the government comes and tells them that such land is theirs. No. It tells them that, if they prove ownership of 2 hectares, they will be given financial support. But where do those 2 hectares come from? Well, from the 'rights-holders'.

In other words, the land that the paper says is one's property has to be broken into pieces for all the applicants. It has to be broken up so that there can be several papers of the same paper (one land title for each applicant). There is no land distribution, there is fragmentation of property. And what happens if the 'rights-holder' doesn't want to or can't? His children want the financial support, but they need the paper. Then they fight with the father. The daughters? Not even taken into account, women do not count in the pieces of paper. And children fight to the death against parents. And the children win and with that paper, because the land remains the same and continues to be where it was, they receive their money. With that payment they go into debt, buy something, or get together to pay the coyote to go to the United States. Since they can't afford it, they sell the paper to someone else. They go to work abroad and it turns out that they are earning to pay back those who lent them. Yes, they send remittances to their relatives, but their families use that to pay the debt. After a while, that child returns or is returned. That is if they don't kill him or kidnap him. But he no longer has land, because he sold the paper and now that land belongs to the person who has the paper. So he murdered his father for a paper he no longer has. And then he has to find the payment to buy the paper again.

The population grows, but the land does not grow. There are more papers, but it is only the same area of land. What is going to happen? That right now they are killing each other between rights-holders and applicants, but later they are going to kill each other between applicants. His children are going to fight among themselves, just as he fought against his parents.

For example: you are a rights-holder with 20 hectares and you have, let's say, 4 children. It is the first generation. You distribute the land or rather the paper and there is now a 5-hectare paper for each one. Then those 4 children have four other children each, second generation, and they distribute their 5 hectares and they get a little more than one hectare each. Then those 4 grandchildren have another 4 children each, third generation, and they divide the paper and each one gets about a quarter of a hectare. Then those great-grandchildren have 4 children each, fourth generation, and they divide the paper and they get a tenth of a hectare each. And I no longer continue, because just in 40 years, in the second generation, they are going to kill each other. That's what bad governments are doing: they are sowing death.

The Old New Road

What has what they call the "material basis" been like in our history of struggle?

Well, first was the food. With the recovery of the lands that were in the hands of the large landowners, the diet improved. Hunger was no longer the guest in our homes. Then, with the autonomy and support of people who are "good people," we say, health followed. Here the support of the fraternal doctors was and is very important, which is what we call them because they are like our brothers who help us not only with serious illnesses. Also, and, above all, in training, that is, in health knowledge. Then education. Then the work on the land. Then what is the government and administration of the Zapatista people themselves. Then what is government and peaceful coexistence with those who are not Zapatistas.

The material basis of this, that is, the mode of production is a coexistence of individual-family work with collective work. Collective work made it possible for the compañeros to participate in autonomy.

Let's say that the first 10 years of autonomy, that is, from the uprising to the birth of the Juntas de Buen Gobierno, in 2003, were years of learning. The next 10 years, until 2013, were about learning the importance of generational change. From 2013 up to date it has been about verifying, criticizing and self-criticizing errors in operation, administration and ethics.

In what follows now, we will have a stage of learning and readjustment. In other words, we will have many errors and problems, because there is no manual or book that tells you how to do it. We will have many falls, yes, but we will get up again and again to continue walking. That is, we are Zapatistas.

The material basis or production basis of this stage will be a combination of individual-family work, collective work and this new thing that we call "communal territory" or "non-ownership."

Individual-family work is based on small and individual or family property. A person and his/her family work their piece of land, their little store, their mobile phone, their livestock. The profit or benefit is for that family.

Collective work is based on the agreement between compañeros to do work on collective land (assigned before the war and expanded after the war). Work is distributed according to time, capacity and disposition. The gain or benefit is for the collective. It is usually used for fiestas, mobilizations, acquisition of health equipment, training of health and education promoters, and for the transportation and maintenance of authorities and autonomous commissions.

The common work begins, now, in tenure of land. A portion of the recovered lands are declared as "communal territory." That is, it is not parceled out and is not owned by anyone, neither small, nor medium, nor large property. That land belongs to no one, it has no owner. And, in agreement with nearby communities, they "lend" each other that land to work on. It cannot be sold or bought. It cannot be used for the production, transfer or consumption of narcotics. The work is done in "shifts" agreed upon with the GALs and the non-Zapatista brothers. The benefit or gain is for those who work, but the property is not, it is a non-property that is used in common. It doesn't matter if you are Zapatista, 'partidista,' Catholic, evangelical, Presbyterian, atheist, Jewish, Muslim, black, white, dark, yellow, red, woman, man, 'otroa.' You can work the land in common, with the agreement of the GALs, CGAL and ACGAL, by town, region or zone, who are the ones who manage compliance with the rules of common use. Everything that serves the common good, nothing that goes against the common good.

What comes next? Well, everyone builds their idea, their thinking, their plan of what is best. And each person perhaps has a different thought and a different way. And that must be respected. Because it is in organized practice where everyone sees what works and what doesn't. In other words, there are no recipes or manuals, because what works for one may not work for another. The global "common" is the sharing of stories, of knowledge, of struggles. In other words, as they say, the journey for life continues. That is, for the struggle.

From the mountains of the Mexican Southeast.

Subcommander Insurgent Moisés.

Mexico, December 2023. 500, 40, 30, 20, 10, 3, a year, a few months, a few weeks, a few days, just a while ago. After.

P.S. — At the end of the interview and after he had checked whether the meaning of his explanations was complete and correct, Subcommander Insurgent Moisés — who received command became the Zapatista spokesperson 10 years ago, in 2013 — lit the umpteenth cigarette. I lit the pipe. We stood looking at the lintel of the 'champa' door. Early morning gave way to dawn and the first lights of day woke up the sounds in the mountains of southeastern Mexico. We didn't say more, but maybe we both thought: "and what's missing is yet to come."

P.S. DECLARED UNDER OATH. — At no moment or stage of the deliberation that led to the decision made by the Zapatista peoples, did quotes or footnotes or references, even distant ones, come to light from Marx, Engels, Lenin, Trotsky, Stalin, Mao, Bakunin, Che, Fidel Castro, Kropotkin, Flores Magón, the Bible, the Koran, Milton Freidman, Milei, progressivism (if it has any bibliographical reference other than its 'charlatans'), Liberation Theology, Lombardo, Revueltas, Freud, Lacan, Foucault, Deleuze, whatever is fashionable or fashionable on the left, or any source from the left, right, or from the non-existent centers. Not only, I also know that they have not read any of the founding works of the isms that fuel the dreams and defeats of the left. For my part, I give unsolicited advice to those who read these lines: everyone is free to make a fool of themselves, but I would recommend that before starting with their nonsense like "the Lacandona laboratory," "the Zapatista experiment," and to categorize this in one sense or another, they think about it a little. Because, speaking of ridiculous, they have already been making a big deal for almost 30 years by "explaining" Zapatismo. Maybe you don't remember now, but what's left over here, in addition to dignity and mud, is memory. Sorry.

I attest

—The Captain

Notes

1   The same person, originally known by the *nom de guerre* of Subcomandante Marcos, and later Subcomandante Galeano, currently goes by the name of Captain Marcos, having been (voluntarily) reduced in military rank and recovering his original *nom de guerre*.

2   A visit to the "Europe of Below" made in 2021 by a Zapatista delegation.

Bibliography

Agosto, Patricia (2006). *El zapatismo: hacia una transformación cooperativa «digna y rebelde»*. Caracas, Monte Ávila Editores Latinoamericanos.

Altmann, Philipp (2013). Interculturalidad y plurinacionalidad como conceptos decoloniales - Colonialidad y discurso del movimiento indígena en el Ecuador. *XV Encuentro de Latinoamericanistas Españoles*, Nov 2012, Madrid, España, pp.131–138.

Aubry, Andrés et al. (2003). *Los Acuerdos de San Andrés*. Edición Bilingüe español-chuj. Gobierno del Estado de Chiapas: Centro Estatal de Lenguas, Artes y Literatura Indígena, Secretaría de Pueblos Indios.

Barbosa, Lia Pinheiro (2024). El método del *O'tán-Puy* u *O'tán-Tot* en la ontología política zapatista y la defensa del «territorio en común»: una lucha anticapitalista y antiimperialista. In Lia Pinheiro Barbosa; Alexander Maximilian Hilsenbeck Filho and Thaís Florencio de Aguiar (Orgs.) *Boletín #7 – Zapatismo y Autonomías. Anticapitalismos y narrativas emergentes* (pp. 24-48). Buenos Aires: CLACSO.

Barbosa, Lia Pinheiro (2022). Integração pedagógica da educação camponesa na América Latina: concepções, experiências e sujeitos no enfrentamento do ontocídio e do epistemicídio. *Abatirá - Revista De Ciências Humanas E Linguagens*, 3(5), 30–53.

Barbosa, Lia Pinheiro (2021). *Lajan lajan 'ayatik* or "Walking in Complementary Pairs." In the Zapatista Women's Struggle, *Latin American Perspectives*, 48(5), pp. 04-24.

Barbosa, Lia Pinheiro (2019). O *Popol Wuj* na contemporânea luta indígena mesoamericana, *Tensões Mundiais*, 15, 28, pp. 75–100, Universidade Estadual do Ceará, Brasil.

Barbosa, Lia Pinheiro (2018a). Mulheres Zapatistas e a Pedagogia da Palavra no tecer da outra educação. InAmanda Motta Castro and Rita de Cássia Machado (Orgs.). *Estudos Feministas. Mulheres e Educação Popular* (pp. 25–48). Volume 2. São Paulo: Editora LiberArs.

Barbosa, Lia Pinheiro (2018b). Epistemologias de Nosotras, Feminismos e Teoria da Selva na construção do conhecimento: aportes das mulheres Zapatistas, *Revista Brasileira de Educação do Campo*, 3, 4, pp. 1128–1155.

Barbosa, Lia Pinheiro (2017). Legado e rupturas da Revolução Soviética desde as lutas sociais na América Latina, *Tensões Mundiais*, 13, 24, pp. 107–138, Universidade Estadual do Ceará, Brasil.

Barbosa, Lia Pinheiro (2016). Educação rebelde e autônoma na práxis revolucionária Zapatista. In Eduardo Rebuá and Pedro Silva (Orgs.). *Educação e filosofia da práxis: reflexões de início de século* (pp. 48–79). Rio de Janeiro: Letra Capital.

Barbosa, Lia Pinheiro (2015). *Educación, resistencia y movimientos sociales: la praxis educativo-política de los Sin Tierra y los Zapatistas*. México: LIBRUNAM.

Barbosa, Lia Pinheiro (2014). Educación y lucha autonómica en la Voz Zapatista: aportes de la Pedagogía del Sentir-Ser, Sentir-Pensar, Sentir-Saber, *Revista Educación y Cultura*, 105, pp. 21–27.

Barkin, David; Sánchez, Alejandra (2019). Sujeto revolucionario comunitario: fortaleciendo sociedades post-capitalistas, *Idéias*, 10: 1–4.

Baronnet, Bruno (2012). *Autonomía y educación indígena. Las escuelas zapatistas de la Selva Lacandona de Chiapas*. México. Quito: Abya-Yala.

Baronnet, Bruno (2010). Zapatismo y educación autónoma: de la rebelión a la dignidad indígena, *Sociedade e Cultura*, 2, 13, pp. 247–258.

Baronnet, Bruno, Mora Bayo, Mariana y Stahler-Sholk, Richard. (eds) (2011). *Luchas "muy otras" Zapatismo y autonomía en las comunidades indígenas de Chiapas*. México: CIESAS/UNACH.

Brancaleone, Cássio (2015). *Teoria Social, democracia e autonomia. Uma interpretação da experiência de autogoverno zapatista*. Rio de Janeiro: Azougue Editorial.

Broda, Johanna (2003). El Culto Mexica de los Cerros de la Cuenca de México: apuntes para la discusión sobre los Graniceros. In Beatriz Albores Zárate and Johanna Broda (Coords.). *Graniceros. Cosmovisión y Meteorología Indígenas de Mesoamérica*. (pp. 49–90). Zinacantepec: El Colegio Mexiquense A.C. / Universidad Nacional Autónoma de México.

Burguete Cal y Mayor, Araceli (2005). Una década de autonomías de facto en Chiapas (1994-2004): los límites. In Pablo Dávalos (Comp.). *Pueblos indígenas, Estado y Democracia* (pp. 239–278). Buenos Aires: CLACSO.

Campa Medonza, Víctor (1999). *Las insurrecciones de los pueblos indios de México. La rebelión Zapatista en Chiapas*. Jalisco: Ediciones Cuéllar.

Carrano, Pedro. (2007). Movimento Sem Terra recebe apoio do Exército Zapatista. <https://mst.org.br/2007/06/15/movimento-sem-terra-recebe-apoio-do-exercito-zapatista/>.

Cedillo-Cedillo, Adela (2012). Análisis de la fundación del EZLN en Chiapas desde la perspectiva de la acción colectiva insurgente. *Liminar* 10 (2), pp. 15–34.

Congreso Nacional Indígena (2019). *En defensa de la Madre Tierra. No al tren maya y el corredor transísmico, no a la guardia nacional*. <http://www.congresonacional indigena.org/2019/02/12/en-defensa-de-la-madre-tierra-no-al-tren-maya-y-el-corredor-transismico-no-a-la-guardia-nacional/>.

Coordinadora Arauco-Malleco (CAM). (2022). *Chem Ka Rakiduam. Pensamiento y Acción de la CAM*. Chile: Coordinadora Arauco-Malleco.

de la Peña Martínez, Luís (2003). Somos el silencio que habla: del oxímoron a la retórica del silencio en el discurso zapatista. *Versión*, 13, 121–139.

EZLN (2024). *Adagios*. <https://enlacezapatista.ezln.org.mx/2024/08/16/adagios-2/>.

EZLN (2023a). *Comunicado EZLN ⊠ Tercera Parte: Dení*, <https://enlacezapatista.ezln.org.mx/2023/11/02/tercera-parte-deni/>.

EZLN (2023b). *Catorceava Parte y Segunda Alerta de Aproximación: La (otra) Regla del Tercero Excluido*. <https://enlacezapatista.ezln.org.mx/2023/11/28/catorceava-parte-y-segunda-alerta-de-aproximacion-la-otra-regla-del-tercero-excluido/>.

EZLN (2023c). *Novena Parte: La Nueva Estructura de la Autonomía Zapatista*. <https://enlacezapatista.ezln.org.mx/2023/11/12/novena-parte-la-nueva-estructura-de-la-autonomia-zapatista/>.

EZLN (2023d). *Vigésima y Última Parte: el Común y la No Propiedad.*
    <https://enlacezapatista.ezln.org.mx/2023/12/20/vigesima-y-ultima-
    parte-el-comun-y-la-no-propiedad/>.

EZLN (2023e). *Ninth Part: The new structure of Zapastista Autonomy.* Nov. 13.
    <https://enlacezapatista.ezln.org.mx/2023/11/13/ninth-part-the-new-structure-
    of-zapastista-autonomy/>.

EZLN (2023f). *Tenth Part: Regarding pyramids and their uses and customary regimes.*
    Nov. 15.
    <https://enlacezapatista.ezln.org.mx/2023/11/15/tenth-part-regarding-pyramids-
    and-their-uses-and-customary-regimes/>.

EZLN (2023g). *Twentieth and Last Part: The Common and Non-Property.* Dec. 22.
    <https://enlacezapatista.ezln.org.mx/2023/12/22/twentieth-and-last-part-the-
    common-and-non-property/>.

EZLN (2020). *Diversos colectivos promueven acción virtual contra proyecto de despojo
    nombrado tren maya.* <https://enlacezapatista.ezln.org.mx/2020/05/12/diversos-
    colectivos-promueven-accion-virtual-contra-el-proyecto-de-despojo-nombrado-
    tren-maya/>.

EZLN (2019). *Palabras del CCRI-CG del EZLN a los pueblos Zapatistas en el 25
    Aniversario del inicio de la Guerra contra el Olvido.* <https://enlacezapatista.ezln.
    org.mx/2019/01/01/palabras-de-la-comandancia-general-del-ejercito-zapatista-
    de-liberacion-nacional-dirigidas-a-los-pueblos-zapatistas/>.

EZLN (2018a). *300. Primera parte: una finca, un mundo, una guerra, pocas
    probabilidades.* Subcomandante Insurgente Moisés. SupGaleano,
    <https://enlacezapatista.ezln.org.mx/2018/08/20/300-primera-parte-
    una-finca-un-mundo-una-guerra-pocas-probabilidades-subcomandante-
    insurgente-moises-supgaleano/>.

EZLN (2018b). *300. Segunda parte: Un continente como patio trasero, un país como
    cementerio, un pensamiento único como Programa de Gobierno, y una pequeña, muy
    pequeña, pequeñísima rebeldía.* Subcomandante Insurgente Moisés. SupGaleano.
    <https://enlacezapatista.ezln.org.mx/2018/08/21/300-segunda-parte-un-
    continente-como-patio-trasero-un-pais-como-cementerio-un-pensamiento-
    unico-como-programa-de-gobierno-y-una-pequena-muy-pequena-pequenisima-
    rebeldia-subcomandante-insurgent/>.

EZLN (2018c). *300. Tercera y última parte: un desafío, una autonomía real,
    una respuesta, varias propuestas, y algunas anécdotas sobre el número "300."*
    Subcomandante Insurgente Moisés. SupGaleano. <https://enlacezapatista.ezln.
    org.mx/2018/08/22/300-tercera-y-ultima-parte-un-desafio-una-autonomia-real-
    una-respuesta-varias-propuestas-y-algunas-anecdotas-sobre-el-numero-300-
    subcomandante-insurgente-moises-supgaleano/>.

EZLN (2015a). *El Pensamiento Crítico Frente a la Hidra Capitalista I. Participación de la
    Comisión Sexta del EZLN,* México.

EZLN (2015b). *Segundo Nivel Escuela Zapatista.* <http://enlacezapatista.ezln.org.
    mx/2015/07/27/segundo-nivel-escuela-zapatista/>.

EZLN (2013a). *Gobierno Autónomo I. Cuaderno de Texto del primer grado del curso "La
    Libertad según l@s Zapatistas.* México.

EZLN (2013b). Gobierno Autónomo II. Cuaderno de textos de primer grado del curso de "La Libertad según l@s Zapatistas." Cuaderno de textos de primer grado del curso de "La Libertad según l@s Zapatistas." México

EZLN (2013c). Participación de las mujeres en el Gobierno Autónomo. Cuaderno de textos de primer grado del curso de "La Libertad según l@s Zapatistas."

EZLN (2013d). Resistencia Autónoma. Cuaderno de textos de primer grado del curso de "La Libertad según l@s Zapatistas."

EZLN (2013e). Ellos y Nosotros. IV. Las Miradas. 1 - Mirar para imponer o mirar para escuchar. <https://enlacezapatista.ezln.org.mx/2013/02/06/ellos-y-nosotros-vilas-miradas/>.

EZLN (2012). Comunicado del Comité Clandestino Revolucionario Indígena - Comandancia General del Ejército Zapatista de Liberación Nacional. 21 de diciembre del 2012. <https://enlacezapatista.ezln.org.mx/2012/12/21/comunicado-del-comite-clandestino-revolucionario-indigena-comandancia-general-del-ejercito-zapatista-de-liberacion-nacional-del-21-de-diciembre-del-2012/>.

EZLN (2007a). Palabras del Teniente Coronel Insurgente Moisés. Mesa redonda en el CIDECI. <http://enlacezapatista.ezln.org.mx/2007/07/20/mesa-redonda-en-elcideci-san-cristobal-de-las-casas/>.

EZLN (2007b). Mesa Redonda en el CIDECI, San Cristóbal de las Casas, 19 de julio de 2007. Palabras del Comandante Tacho. < https://enlacezapatista.ezln.org.mx/2007/07/20/mesa-redonda-en-el-cideci-san-cristobal-de-las-casas/#tacho>.

EZLN (2007c). EZLN: apoyo a la Campaña Mundial en defensa de la tierra y el territorio. <https://www.biodiversidadla.org/Noticias/EZLN_apoyo_a_la_Campana_Mundial_en_defensa_de_la_tierra_y_el_territorio>.

EZLN (2006). Arte en Rebeldía. México: Ediciones Rebeldía.

EZLN (1998a). Fuerte es su corazón: los municipios rebeldes zapatistas. México.

EZLN (1998b). Quinta Declaración de la Selva Lacandona. <https://enlacezapatista.ezln.org.mx/1998/07/17/v-declaracion-de-la-selva-lacandona/>.

EZLN (1996). Crónicas intergalácticas – EZLN. Primer Encuentro Intercontinental por la Humanidad y contra el Neoliberalismo. Chiapas: Estampas Artes Gráficas.

EZLN (1995a). Tercera Declaración de la Selva Lacandona. <https://enlacezapatista.ezln.org.mx/1995/01/01/tercera-declaracion-de-la-selva-lacandona/>.

EZLN (1995b). EZLN. Documentos y Comunicados 2 - 15 de agosto de 1994/ 29 de septiembre de 1995. México: Ediciones ERA.

EZLN (1994). Segunda Declaración de la Selva Lacandona. <https://enlacezapatista.ezln.org.mx/1994/06/10/segunda-declaracion-de-la-selva-lacandona/>.

EZLN (s/f). Había una vez una noche. ESRAZ - Escuela Secundaria Rebelde Autónoma Zapatista Primer de Enero. Caracol II - Oventik, Chiapas, México.

Esteva, Gustavo (2014). Nuevas formas de la revolución. Apuntes para pensar las luchas del EZLN y la APPO. México: Cooperativa El Rebozo.

Fernández Christieb, Paulina (2014). Justicia Autónoma Zapatista. Zona Selva Tzeltal. México: Ediciones Autónom@s.

Freire, Paulo (1987). Pedagogia do Oprimido. Rio de Janeiro: Paz e Terra.

Fuentes Sánchez, Waldo Lao (2022). La lucha no es por el poder, sino un llamado a la organización de los pueblos. María de Jesús Patricia Martínez, primera mujer indígena por la candidatura presidencial en México. *Brazilian Journal of Latin American Studies*, 21(42), pp. 63–85.

Galindo, María (2013). *No se puede descolonizar sin despatriarcalizar. Teoría y propuesta de la despatriarcalización*. Bolivia: Mujeres Creando.

García de León, Antonio (1995). La vuelta del Katún (Chiapas: a veinte años del Primer Congreso Indígena), *Revista Chiapas* 1, 127–147, Universidad Nacional Autónoma de México, México.

Gómez Lara, Horacio (2011). *Indígenas, mexicanos y rebeldes. Procesos educativos y resignificación de identidades en los Altos de Chiapas*. México: Juan Pablo Editor.

González Casanova, Pablo (2009a). *De la sociología del poder a la sociología de la explotación. Pensar América Latina en el Siglo XXI*. Bogotá: Siglo del Hombre Editores / Buenos Aires: CLACSO Coediciones.

González Casanova, Pablo (2009b). El saber y el conocer de los pueblos. *Primer Coloquio Internacional In Memoriam Andrés Aubry*. San Cristóbal de las Casas: Cideci Unitierra Ediciones, pp. 293–316.

González Casanova, Pablo (2003). Los "Caracoles" Zapatistas: redes de resistencia y autonomía, *Memoria*, 176, pp. 14–19.

González Casanova, Pablo (05 de marzo de 1997). La Teoría de la Selva. Contra el neoliberalismo y por la humanidad (Proyecto de Intertexto), *La Jornada*. <jornada.com.mx/1997/03/06/perfil.html>.

González Casanova, Pablo (04 de septiembre de 1995). Causas de la rebelión de Chiapas, *La Jornada*.

González, Miguel. (2010). Autonomías territoriales indígenas y regímenes autonómicos (desde el Estado) en América Latina. In Miguel González, Araceli Burguete Cal and Mayor y Pablo Ortiz-T. (coords.). *La autonomía a debate: Autogobierno indígena y Estado plurinacional en América Latina* (pp. 35–62). Quito: Flacso.

Guerrero Martínez, Fernando (2022). *Yaltsil. Vida, ambiente y persona en la cosmovisión tojol-ab'al*. Chiapas: LIBRUNAM.

Gunderson, Christopher (2017). The communist roots of Zapatismo and the Zapatista uprising. *Perspectives on Global Development and Technology*, 16(1-3), pp. 167–179.

Kouachi, Rawiya (2018). Eloquent Silences in Samuel Beckett's *Waiting for Godot* and Harold Pinter's *The Dumb Waiter*, *AWEJ for Translation & Literary Studies*, 2(1), pp. 172.–181.

Krenak, Ailton (2024). *Futuro ancestral*. Rio de Janeiro: Taurus.

La Jornada (02 de enero de 2020). *"Hasta morir si es preciso", luchará el EZLN contra los megaproyectos*. <https://jornada.com.mx/2020/01/02/politica/006n1pol#:~:text= Morelia%2C%20Altamirano%2C%20Chis.%2C%20Al%20cumplirse%2026%20a%C3% B1os%20de,la%20que%20defenderemos%20hasta%20morir%20si%20es%20preciso>.

Le Bot, Yvon (1997). *Subcomandante Marcos - el sueño Zapatista*. Barcelona: Crónica Anagrama.

Lenkersdorf, Carlos (2008). *Aprender a escuchar. Enseñanzas maya-tojolabales*. México: Plaza y Valdés.

Lenkersdorf, Carlos (2005). *Los hombres verdaderos. Voces y testimonios tojolabales*. México, Siglo XXI.

Lenkersdorf, Carlos (2004). *Conceptos tojolabales de filosofía y del altermundo*. México: Plaza y Valdés.

Lenkersdorf, Carlos (2002). *Filosofar en Clave Tojolabal*. México, Editora Porrúa.

López Intzín, Juan (2013). Ich'el ta muk: la trama de la construcción del lekil kuxlejal (vida plena-digna-justa). In Georgina Méndéz Torres.; Juan López Intzín; Sylvia Marcos and Carmen Osorio Hernández (Coords.). *Senti-pensar el género: perspectivas desde los pueblos originarios*. (pp. 101-110). Guadalaja: Red IIPIM / Red de Feminismos Decoloniales / Taller Editorial La Casa del Mago.

López y Rivas, Gilberto (2020). *Pueblos indígenas en tiempos de la Cuarta Transformación*. Ciudad de México: Bajo Tierra.

Ley Revolucionaria de Mujeres (1993). *El Despertador Mexicano, Órgano Informativo del EZLN*, México, No.1, diciembre. https://enlacezapatista.ezln.org. mx/1993/12/31/ley-revolucionaria-de-mujeres/

Machín Sosa, Braulio; Roque Jaime, Adilen María; Ávila Lozano, Dana Rocío y Rosset, Peter Michael. (2010). *Revolución agroecológica: el movimiento de campesino a campesino de la ANAP en Cuba. Cuando el campesino ve, hace fe*. La Habana: ANAP/ La Vía Campesina.

Marcos, Sylvia (2011). *Mujeres, indígenas, rebeldes, zapatistas*. México: Ediciones Eón.

Marcos, Sylvia (2017). Desde abajo: la episteme de la Teología india. In Daniel Inclán; Lucía Linsalatta and Márgara Millán, M. (orgs.). *Modernidades Alternativas* (pp. 155–174). Ciudad de México: Universidad Nacional Autónoma de México.

Martínez Cuero, Julieta. (2022). ¿*Campesinos, indígenas y migrantes? Articulación de distintos modos de producción en Los Altos de Chiapas*. Ciudad de México: Universidad Autónoma Metropolitana.

Martínez Cuero, Julieta (2013). Articulación y/o confrontación de distintos modos de producción en Los Altos de Chiapas. Tesis de Doctorado. Posgrado en Estudios Sociales. México: Universidad Autónoma Metropolitana.

Millán, Márgara (2014). *Des-Ordenando el Género / Descentrando la nación? El Zapatismo de las mujeres indígenas y sus consecuencias*. México: UNAM/ Ediciones del Lirio.

Millán, Márgara (1996). Las zapatistas de fin de milenio. Hacia políticas de autorepresentación de las mujeres indígenas. *Revista Chiapas*, 3, pp. 19–32.

Mora, Mariana (2023). *Kanantayel Lum K'inal*, en la autonomía zapatista. *Revista de la Universidad de México*, 903/904, 56–59.

Mora, Mariana (2017). *Kuxlejal Politics: Indigenous Autonomy, Race, and Decolonizing Research in Zapatista Communities*. Austin: University of Texas.

Movimento dos Trabalhadores Rurais Sem Terra (2007). *Movimento Sem Terra recebe apoio do Exército Zapatista*. <https://mst.org.br/2007/06/15/movimento-sem-terra-recebe-apoio-do-exercito-zapatista/>.

Narváez Gutiérrez, Raúl (2005). Educación y zapatismo entre los tsotsiles: entre la asimilación y la resistencia. Análisis de proyectos de educación básica oficiales y autónomos. Tesis de Maestría. CIESAS – Centro de Investigaciones y Estudios Superiores en Antropología Social.

Palabra (2011). <https://enlacezapatista.ezln.org.mx/>.

Paoli, Antonio (2005). *Educación, autonomía y lekil kuxlejal. Aproximaciones sociolingüísticas a la sabiduría de los tzeltales*. México: Universidad Autónoma Metropolitana.

Pérez Moreno, María Patricia (2021). *Stael o modo de ser, pensar, hacer, sentir, vivir del pueblo Tseltal de Bachajón*. In Xóchitl Leyva Sollano; Lola Cubels Aguilar and Júnia M. Trigueiro de Lima (Coords.). *Sistemas normativos y prácticas autonómicas del pueblo tzeltal de Chilón y Silalá*. (pp. 37–47). Cidade do México: Centro de Derechos Humanos Miguel Agustín Pro Juárez.

Pérez Moreno, María Patricia (2019). *O'tanil:* corazón. Una sabiduría y práctica de sentir, pensar, entender, explicar y vivir el mundo desde los mayas tzeltales de Bachajón, Chiapas, México. In Karina Ochoa Muñoz (Coord.). *Miradas en torno al problema colonial. Pensamiento anticolonial y feminismos descoloniales en los Sures Globales.* (pp. 157–173). México: Akal.

Pitarch Ramón, Pedro (1996). *Ch'ulel. Una etnografía de las almas tzeltales.* México: Fondo de Cultura Económica.

Rajchenberg, Enrique y Catheryne Héau-Lambert. (2004). Los silencios zapatistas. *Revista Chiapas,* 16: pp. 1–11.

Rivera Cusicanqui, Silvia (2004). La noción de "derecho" o las paradojas de la modernidad postcolonial: indígenas y mujeres en Bolivia, *Aportes Andinos,* 11, pp. 01–15.

Rosset, Peter Michael (2007). "La guerra por la tierra y el territorio", en *Primero Coloquio Internacional inmemoriam Andrés Aubry.* San Cristóbal de las Casas: Universidad de la Tierra, Rebeldía.

Rosset, Peter, and Miguel A. Altieri (2017). *Agroecology: Science and Politics.* Halifax, NS: Fernwood.

Rosset, Peter Michael, María Elena Martínez-Torres and Luis Hernández-Navarro (2005). Zapatismo in the Movement of Movements. *Development,* 48, 2, pp. 35–41.

Rosset, Peter Michael, and María Elena Martínez-Torres (2016). Agroecología, territorio, recampesinización y movimientos sociales, *Estudios Sociales,* 25, 47, pp. 275–299.

Saénz Boldt, Charlotte Marie, Lia Pinheiro Barbosa and Tania Cruz Salazar (2021). Pedagógica de Semilla en el Movimiento Zapatista: siembra y crecimiento de un sujeto político colectivo, *Práxis Educacional,* 17, 46, pp. 01–24.

Sánchez Ramírez, José Luís (2018). Los silencios colectivos como acción política utilizados por el EZLN. In Juan Carlos Ruiz Guadalajara y Gustavo A. Urbina Cortés (Coords.) *Acción colectiva, movimientos sociales, sociedad civil y participación* (pp. 580–596). *Vol. II.* México: COMECSO.

Segato, Rita Laura (2014). *Las nuevas formas de la guerra y el cuerpo de las mujeres.* México: Editorial Pez en el Árbol.

Shivji, Issa G. (2017). The Concept of 'Working People.' *Agrarian South: Journal of Political Economy,* 6, 1, pp. 01–13.

Stahler-Sholk, Richard (2007). Resisting neoliberal homogenization: The Zapatista Autonomy Movement. *Latin American Perspectives,* 34, 2, pp. 48–63.

Starr, Amory, María Elena Martínez-Torres and Peter Michael Rosset (2011). Participatory democracy in action: Practices of the Zapatistas and the Movimento Sem Terra. *Latin American Perspectives,* 38, 1, pp. 102–119.

Subcomandante Insurgente Marcos (2007). Ni el centro, ni la periferia ... Parte VII (y última) – sentir el rojo. El calendario y la geografía de la Guerra," en *Primero Coloquio Internacional inmemoriam Andrés Aubry.* San Cristóbal de las Casas: Universidad de la Tierra, Rebeldía.

Subcomandante Insurgente Marcos (21 de julho de 2003). Chiapas: La Treceava Estela. *Enlace Zapatista, Archivo Histórico*. <https://enlacezapatista.ezln.org.mx/2003/07/21/chiapas-la-treceava-estela-primera-parte-un-caracol/>.

Subcomandante Insurgente (2017). *Kamegusha: Abril también es mañana*. <https://enlacezapatista.ezln.org.mx/2017/04/12/kagemusha-abril-tambien-es-manana/>.

The Mixed Space. n.d. 7 Principles of Zapatismo to Consider in Community Building. Blog. <https://www.themixedspace.com/7-principles-of-zapatismo-to-consider-in-community-building/>.

Val, Valentín, y Peter Michael Rosset (2022). *Agroecología(s) emancipatoria(s) para un mundo donde florezcan muchas autonomías*. Buenos Aires / Guadalajara: CLACSO / Universidad de Guadalajara.

zz colectivo. 2012. *"El derecho de ser feliz" - Encuentro de las Mujeres Zapatistas con las Mujeres del Mundo*. Video-Documental sobre el "1er Encuentro de las Mujeres Zapatistas con las Mujeres del Mundo" en diciembre de 2007 y enero de 2008 en La Garrucha, Chiapas / México, 39 minutes. <https://youtu.be/aWkKwdGKtxE>.

Index